The Heart of a Poet

Words for a Better Tomorrow

The Conscious Poets

inner child press international

General Information

The Heart of a Poet
Words for a Better Tomorrow

1ˢᵗ Edition: 2020

This Publishing is protected under Copyright Law as a "Collection". All rights for all submissions are retained by the individual author and / or artist. No part of this publishing may be reproduced, transferred in any manner without the prior *WRITTEN CONSENT* of the "Material Owner" or its Representative, Inner Child Press. Any such violation infringes upon the Creative and Intellectual Property of the Owner pursuant to International and Federal Copyright Law. Any queries pertaining to this "Collection" should be addressed to Publisher of Record.

Publisher Information:

Inner Child Press
intouch@innerchildpress.com
www.innerchildpress.com

This Collection is protected under U.S. and International Copyright Laws

Copyright © 2020: Inner Child Press

ISBN-13: 978-1-952081-23-1 (inner child press, ltd.)

$ 24.95

Table of Contents

A Few Words from the Publisher   ix
Disclaimer   xi

The Poetry ~ Words for a Better Tomorrow

Roy Austin	3
Eliza Segiet	5
Sridevi Selvaraj	7
Rickey K. Hood	9
Gopal Lahiri	11
Rubab Abdullah	13
Rosemarie Wilson	15
Denis Popov	17
Bhagya Senaratne	19
Mark Andrew Heathcote	21
June Barefield	23
Shernaz Wadia	26
Ayo Ayoola-Amale	28
Pentecost Mate	30
Jyotirmaya Thakur	33
Brenda Mohammed	35
Faleeha Hassan	37
Iwu Jeff	39
Tali Cohen Shabtai	41
Anwer Ghani	43
Florin Ciocea	45
Debbi Brody	47
Setaluri Padmavathi	49
Padmaja Iyengar-Paddy	51

Table of Contents... *continued*

Santosh Bakaya	53
B. S. Tyagi	55
Rahim Karim	58
Ashok Chakravarthy Tholana	60
Sujata Dash	62
Thryaksha A. Garla	64
Khalid Imam	66
Suma K. Gopal	68
Menduh Leka	70
Pushmaotee Subrun	72
Ranjana Sharan Sinha	75
Hema Ravi	77
Louise Hudon	79
Sameer Goel	82
Somasuntharampillai Pathmanathan	84
Zinia Mitra	87
Kwame MA McPherson	89
T. Sree Latha	91
Akshaya Kumar Das	93
Rita Stanzione	95
'Siv'	97
Avijit Roy	99
Sahaj Sabharwal	101
Dilip Mohapatra	103
Bhisma Upreti	105
Otteri Selvakumar	107
Jodel E. Agbayani	109
Shareef Abdur-Rasheed	111

Table of Contents... *continued*

Lilla Latus	113
Umasree Raghunath	115
Varsha Das	118
Akash Sagar Chouhan	122
Hayim Abramson	124
Tom Higgins	126
Warda Zerguine	128
Maria do Sameiro Barroso	130
Aziz Mountassir	132
Elizabeth Kurian	134
Hussein Habasch	136
Nguyen Chau Ngoc Doan Chinh	138
Neelam Saxena Chandra	141
Ashok Bhargava	143
Avril Meallem	145
Kamar Sultana Sheik	147
Sujan Bhattacharyya	150
Aditi Roy	152
Gino Leineweber	154
Zaldy Carreon De Leon, Jr.	156
Aneek Chatterjee	159
Shruti Goswami	161
Chijioke Ogbuike	163
Lucky Stephen Onyah	165
Izza Fartmis	167
Mamu Roshid	169
Kamala Wijeratne	171
Kapardeli Eftichia	173

Table of Contents ... *continued*

Olfa Philo Drid	176
Orbindu Ganga	180
Basab Mondal	182
Phuntsho Wangchuk	184
Divya Sinha	186
Anuradha Bhattacharyya	188
Sunil Sharma	190
Tzemin Ition Tsai	192
S. Sundar Rajan	194
Jyoti Kanetkar	196
Kamani Jayasekera	198
Kimberly Burnham	200
Ibrahim Honjo	202
Alicia Minjarez Ramirez	204
Monsif Beroual	206
Tyran Prizren Spahiu	208
Iram Fatima 'Ashi'	210
Shubha Khandekar	212
K. Pankajam	214
Gita Bharath	216
Annapurna Sharma A.	218
Sumita Dutta Shoam	221
Ndaba Sibanda	224
Gobinda Biswas	226
Yuan Changming	228
Welkin Siskin	230
Ashrit Mohapatra	232
Luzviminda G. Rivera	234

Table of Contents ... *continued*

Nutan Sarawagi	236
K. Radhakrishnan	241
Smruti Ranjan Mohanty	243
Vidya Shankar	246
Sudarsan Sahu	249
John Eliot	251
Alicja Maria Kuberska	253
Fahredin Shehu	255
Preety Sengupta	257
Ahila	259
Claudia Piccinno	261
Maryam Abbasi	263
Andrew Scott	265
Paramita Mukherjee Mullick	267
Eden Soriano Trinidad	269
Anna Nicole D. Velez	271
Awatef El Idrissi Boukhris	273
Fethi Sassi	276
Ashok Kumar	278
Ana María Manuel Rosa	280
Debaprasanna Biswas	283
Lily Swarn	285
Valerie Ames	287
Sayeed Abubakar	289
Akhmad Cahyo Setio	291
Farooq Ahmad Sheikh	293
Elizabeth Esguerra Castillo	296
Madhumathi	298

Table of Contents ... *continued*

Seena Sreevalson	301
Nirmal Jaswal	303
Noreen Ann Snyder	305
Zia Marshall	307
Hatmiati Masy'ud	309
Mallika Chari	311
Shamayita Sen	313
Tara Andaru Noesantara	315
Queen Sarkar	317
Teresa E. Gallion	319
Muhammad Azram	321
Fernando Martinez Alderete	323
Yanz Haryo Darmista	325
Asoke Kumar Mitra	327
Kay Salady	329
Ameedah Mawalin	331
Nandita De nee Chatterjee	333
Sylvia L. Blalock	336
hülya n. yılmaz	338
William S. Peters, Sr.	340

A Few Words from the Publisher

Poetry is a sacred and an authentic art form that has travelled throughout time. From the first guttural utterances of mankind, there was a rhythm that inebriated the senses, the minds, the hearts and souls of all who had an ear to hear.

Our aim at Inner Child Press International is to participate in this tradition and offer a consciousness to the world from the poet's perspective. As a poet / writer myself, I realize that my words are an embodiment of many aspects of my experience and my existence. There are the issues that are set deep within my core, albeit love, social observance and / or critique as well as the many matters that affect my spirit. Our mission here at Inner Child Press International is to share with the world an inclusive vision as seen by the contributors who are in this volume of poetic consciousness. Take the time and read some of the thoughts, contemplations and feelings of the 'Poets for Humanity' from across the globe.

Bless Up

Bill

Publisher
Inner Child Press International
'building bridges of cultural understanding'
www.innerchildpress.com

Disclaimer

In our attempts to maintain the integrity of the poets' voices in the publication before you, *The Heart of a Poet*, we have elected to do minimal surface editing. We felt that preserving the original entries was critically important for you, the reader, to enjoy each poem's authenticity.

You may encounter a few challenges in achieving total clarity of the messages shared through poetry, but I indulge you to let go of your critical thinking and embrace the spirit through words offered 'for a better tomorrow'.

From the desk of

hülya n. yılmaz, Ph.D.
Director of Editing

Inner Child Press International
'building bridges of cultural understanding'

The Heart of a Poet

Words for a Better Tomorrow

The Heart of a Poet

Roy Austin is retired, and lives in Dorset, England. He enjoys rural pursuits and walking his Labrador. He also writes poetry and various articles that point towards sage teachings. T. S. Eliot once wrote, "Our lot crawls between dry ribs, to keep our metaphysics warm". Roy is in empathy with that poetic sentiment.

The Child

Ivy of course, climbs
the strength of the bole,

branching up into
existence, both are

reaching for the light,
the whole canopy,

both pay the price, a
tangled sacrifice,

to live together
in growing as one,

both prematurely
fall down and are done;

every time I see
in the sylvan wild

in minute locus,
a curious child

with closer focus,
that could not reach or

even show, how it
had much to teach me.

Eliza Segiet has an M.A. in Philosophy and a postgraduate degree in Cultural Knowledge, Philosophy, Arts and Literature from the Jagiellonian University. Her poems, "Questions" and "Sea of Mists" won the International Publication of the Year in 2017 and 2018 from Spillwords Press. She has been nominated for the 2019 Pushcart Prize, the 2020 Naji Naaman Literary Prize and the 2020 iWoman Global Awards. Her poetry can be found in anthologies and literary magazines worldwide.

Hope

Hidden
behind Stone Boulders,
written on pages
songs of souls
waiting to be fulfilled.
Catharsis of thoughts,
the pleading words of hope.

On the hill of Moriah
nobody loses it.

Translated by Artur Komoter

The Heart of a Poet

Sridevi Selvaraj is a bilingual writer. She writes poems and stories in Tamil and English. She has translated the first part of the Tamil classic *Thirukkural* into English.

A Trip Around

I heard the silence of the leaves
They were in meditation, I was told.

I heard the mild storm breathing
Air of blessings on the lovely clouds.

I heard the flower blooming slowly
Bright orange and gold hued well.

I heard the cat dreaming of happiness
It ran around jumping with joy.

I heard the child trusting my fingers
Sleeping in a smooth flowing growth.

I heard the lamp living little by little
Enlightening the shadow around.

I heard the thought of the lover
He knew his trees will soon bloom.

I heard the tears of the mother
They were born out of happiness.

I heard the silent song of Earth
The Mother sang a tune of wisdom.

I heard the quiet acceptance of will
Humanity patiently waited well.

I heard the voice of timelessness
It merged me with the universe.

I heard the happiness of galaxy
Serene being with peace and love.

I sailed and sailed and heard
The melody of life and rhythm.

Rickey K. Hood, is an award-winning poet, essayist, playwright and performer. His poems and essays have appeared in many anthologies, such as *Journey to Timbooktu* (edited by Memphis Vaughan Jr.); *Our Truth* (edited by Dr. Uplift); *Main Street Rag*, Volume 6 #1; *Humanities in the South, Journal of the Southern Humanities Council* #89, and numerous others. He has been honored twice in the *Marquis: Who's Who in America* (2001 and 2002 editions). He has completed his B.A. degree at the University of NC at Charlotte in 2004. He resides in the Washington D.C. metro area.

I Heard God Laughing

While sitting in the park
I heard the laughter of children
Loud and wonderful
Pouring down as rain on budding leaves
And it was then I understood
That it was God I heard laughing.

The soft still voice of the wind
Broke forth in a belly shaking laugh
Filling the air with a pure unconditional joy
A good belly laugh not filled with wrath,
Vengeance, punishments or judgments

I was surprised to hear that is was
Not a "look at man's foolishness" laugh
Or, God is laughing at us, laugh
But instead, God is laughing with us
Enjoying the joy of the day

Now I can hear the happiness of God
Whose laughter rains down on us
Through the joy of children

Gopal Lahiri is a Kolkata-based bilingual poet, critic, editor, translator and writer with 20 books to his credit, including three that were co-authored. 13 of them have been published in English and 7, in Bengali. His poetry has appeared in various anthologies and in eminent journals of India and abroad. His poems have been translated into 8 languages. He has been invited to several poetry festivals across India.

The Allure

Let us open all the glass windows
in the mountains of another time,
the cluster of stars and galaxies wipe out
the anguish and miseries,
a tuft of grass is riffling amid the sea of blades.

Before this vastness, we can still hold
the line of beauty and form within,
in a world as challenging as this one,
sharing the grief and trouble and finally
dance our sorrows away.

There is stillness of the clouds,
music of water and the rock fracture,
capturing the ripples of life,
with an infinite coast lost in the aloofness
yet scripting soul stories.

Strapped in grey surrounds, the distance
between the unheard voices increases,
we expect the light to go in silence,
what to do with the motion of the sea
yet hope glistens from afar.

The soft rays of light rise above,
we feel its warmth of fire.
the birds write copious and rewrite all the time,
everywhere the allure, the aroma wafts in
footsteps recall love and peace in silence.

The Heart of a Poet

Rubab Abdullah, now a citizen of the United States, was born in Dhaka, Bangladesh. She has her higher education from the University of Dhaka. She is a published poet whose work has appeared in many anthologies and newspapers based in Bangladesh and the USA.

The Leading Light

Heartaches won't bother you
Struggles afflict your righteousness so
Yet you let your love adorn all-
How could others feel as deeply as you?
You light up souls of millions,
Offering endlessly your light.

When a distressed soul succumbs
To the sweltering wind of reality,
Feels parched and bare and longs for help
Like the Monsoon you emerge,
Your emotion streams down ceaselessly,
You are the leading light.

You seek release from the bondage of any undue will,
A dissenting voice raises within you.
On hearing shrieks of starved and meagre folks
You exude fellow feeling
You are the leading light!

Rosemarie Wilson, a.k.a. One Single Rose™, is an award-winning poet and playwright, spoken word artist, singer, actress and filmmaker from Detroit. She is currently a featured artist and songwriter with Defected Records – the United Kingdom's #1 house music record label. She is one of the first poets published under the Broadside-Lotus Press merger, two of the oldest African-American publishing companies in the United States. One Single Rose™ performs nationally and internationally wherever her words are welcomed.

www.onesinglerose.com

The Spiked Bandit #19

An invisible thief
crept into the universe . . .
shutting the world DOWN . . .
stealing our breath
from the outside
in . . .
forcing us to batten down separate hatches
on common ground
sheltering in place . . .
streets empty on Wednesday afternoon
like a Sunday morning.
But we sat down,
strong
sending virtual messages of hope
while bouncing off the walls
anxiously awaiting
familial touch –
grandma's hands,
smiling faces,
a firm handshake,
warm embraces
that melt away the pain
of yesterday . . .
We won't ever be the same
but
we'll stand up,
TOGETHER,
STRONGER,
picking up where we left off
when we were forced
to be
still . . .
highs and lows from inside our souls –
hope that Mr. or Mrs. Spiked Bandit #19
THE most notorious thief
no one's ever seen
goes back into hiding
forever . . .

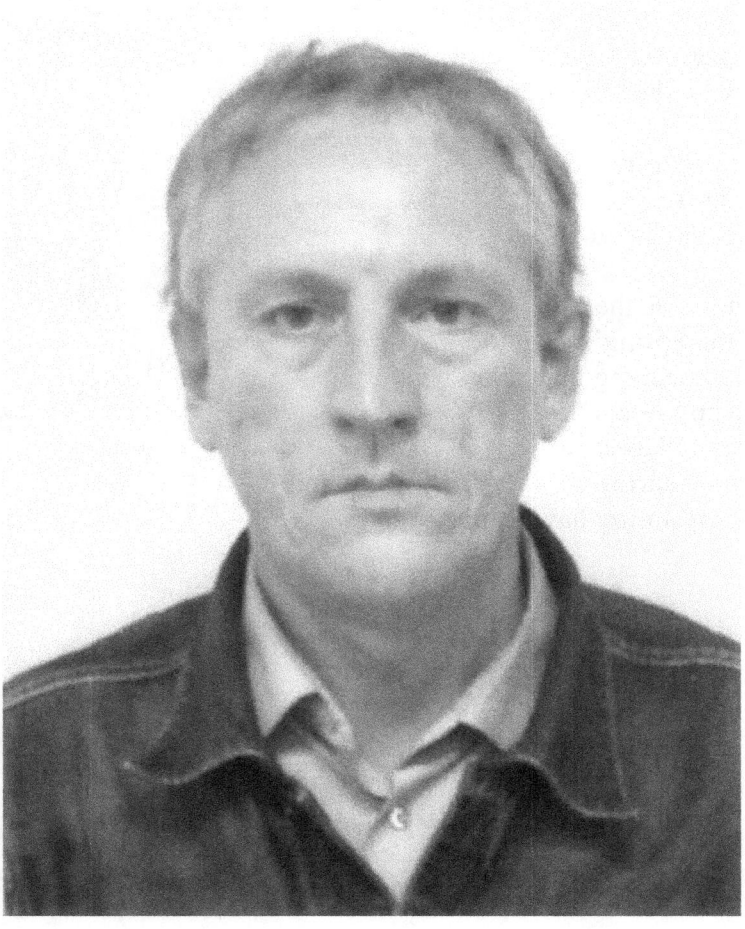

Denis Popov, 48, is a Russian who is working as a teacher of English. He has been writing poems in English throughout his life.

Five Days Before Spring

The winter's almost gone
Its mirror's overturned
The glass is dark
But I can see the days that come
So, anyway, the previous page is burnt
And I will sweep the dust of snow from eyes

Celebration of the Spring
I buried fears under snow
I took my joys and let'em go

Inside my room there is the Sun
Inside my room the Spring's around
I give the wings to sleeping butterflies
It's time to wake up, time to rise
I'll stop to sing my lullabies
Five days before my spring
Five days before my spring have come

Bhagya Senaratne is a lecturer in the Department of Strategic Studies of the General Sir John Kotelawala Defence University, Sri Lanka. She publishes extensively for academic purposes. As creative writing is one of her favourite hobbies, she writes frequently on her blogsite. Her first publication on creative writing is titled *An Experience of a Sri Lankan Child in Japan*.

www.robesofamuse.blogspot.com

Flowing in the Sansarik Journey

Our lives flow in this Sansarik chakra,
I know of this.
Reminiscing old memories and living in the past is unhealthy,
I know this.
I am merely trying to keep afloat,
Not drowning in the deep dark waters that invite me, seduce me.
I do look to the future,
Bright and happy,
Welcoming the immense possibilities ahead of me.
I know this.
I know my mind holds the key,
That my abilities and my youthfulness
Provide me with the stepping stone for this journey.
All this I know and am aware of.
You are right,
There is pain in the pleasure.
Like you, I endure this,
As I tread on my Sansarik journey.

Mark Andrew Heathcote is from Manchester, UK. He began writing poetry at an early age. He has authored two books of poems, *In Perpetuity* and *Back on Earth*, published by Creative Talents Unleashed. Mark is a support worker in adult-learning difficulties.

A Luminary Light Befalls

When shadows drib a luminary light befalls
sweet visions are born filled with aspiration
so it is we should stand tall never be small,
the sun rise's on us all when a new day begins.
It is with the angels & birds our heart sings
don't lose faith, please, hang in there strong-strong-strong
the dark, nights, they're many but hope-always rings
catch me in them falling leaves Lord, lifelong.
Let us soar on high with eagle-talon claws
let me seize my life from dark obscurity,
let us balance on a sword's edge to applause
and love ourselves and others fulsomely.
When shadows drib a luminary light befalls
on butterflies, wings fly straight through them squalls.

The Heart of a Poet

June Barefield is a budding anarchist, military veteran, and a proud father of three. He has authored three collections of poetry, and enjoys reading, the outdoors – mostly sunrises, and makes a swell pot of rice and beans too!

Stay Human

Constantly shifting this ephemeral landscape
The natural process of the rock, waves, wood, the bone and sinew
Sometimes suddenly something is made new
Shape all the faces in a mist of evanescence
A crystalline snowflake shift
Delicate along distant shores delightfully wrapped in the intricate
Again subtly shifting, always changing
Constantly evolving, advancing, becoming human
To be
A human being

The simplest purification's inside heart strings
silent strings
the pure stream
a holy incorruptible ring
a heavenly journey taken by earthbound beings
instinct & intuition
the wilderness & her wisdom
simple things
silent strings
The pure stream fixed on some mysterious cue from the superlative
Then passed down
This life-giving grail and singular beauty
Spectacular
Its radiance fueled and retooled for the marathon ahead, over and again
Endurance uncanny, lacking all but indomitable spirit and agility
Forever evolving inevitably
Call it the migrants cleverly orchestrated connectivity
Connected forever to being
To be
A human being

Here in exists this naive, brilliant, benevolence as a starry night sings an ever-mysterious interplay
The ever illusive, all inclusive, interpolation of the life game, strumming heavenly

heartstrings, urgently slow
And ages go by
Time secretly and serenely engulfs more time
What is time?
In more time still
A third eYe
Connected cosmically to be purified 7even times on this journey earthbound
And sometimes
suddenly
something is made new
shaping the faces while the mist escapes
evolving into truth
The truth of being
To be
A Human Being.

To Shernaz Wadia (from Pune, India), reading and writing poems has been one of the means to embark on an inward journey. She hopes her words will bring peace, hope and light into dark corners. Her poetry has appeared in many Indian and international e-journals and anthologies. She has authored and published *Whispers of the Soul* and two volumes of *Tapestry Poetry – A Fusion of Two Minds*. It is an innovative form of collaborative poetry-writing that she developed and co-authored with Avril Meallem from Israel.

http:/tapestrypoetry.webs.com

A Simple Song

Radiant flowers are in bloom
They counter Corona's dour gloom

Birds tweet as they go for the worm
With zest life's glory they affirm

Doomsayers will paint pictures dark
Shut them out. Take note of the lark

Its song surges with hope and bliss
Our fears purges; naught is amiss

Pure delight suffuses nature
Wellness illumines our future

Hold hurt spirits in faith's firm sling
Let your heart to valour's thrum cling

Sooner or later this will pass
So, to new prospects raise a glass

Ayo Ayoola-Amale is of African heritage. She is acknowledged as a poet for positive social change. She believes that contributing to social change and to progress is very important for poets, but she also thinks that change or advocacy is not the mandatory duty of poets or artists. Ayo enjoys going into schools as a committed advocate of poetry who has seen the critical role that poetry plays as an important catalyst for learning, stimulating creativity and in developing vital communities. In her poems, she concentrates on the problem of violence, racism and the breakdown of human community.

What May We Hope?

We walk on.
We walk on rock bottom.
What may we hope?
We work in hearts
hearing an echo of birds singing on the green hills,
then we sprung to the rays of the rising sun, gleaming,
seeing growing heaven streaming,
seeing a waking dream like sprouting seeds
basking in like a canary bird spreading its wings
soaking in sunshine.
What may we hope?
Holding up the fire,
we rise killing all the dragons in thick muscle winter,
the phoenix rising,
rising in our springtime garden's brightened brow,
rising in the darkest of days with distressing eyes, glow
rising for the possible diamonds, the height of a Masai zebra,
for the possible glory,
for the anything's possible story.
What may we hope?
The stars in the darkness walks briskly on the streets
in search of us to sprout for the moon.
We've decided to keep grace rising
instead of fresh reality becoming blushing agony.
We've decided to keep grace rising,
to keep rising to the sun
with rainbow in our heart
longing for the boundless hugeness of the ocean-
to drown in sweetness like ants swarm on fresh honey.
What may we hope for?

It's all or nothing.

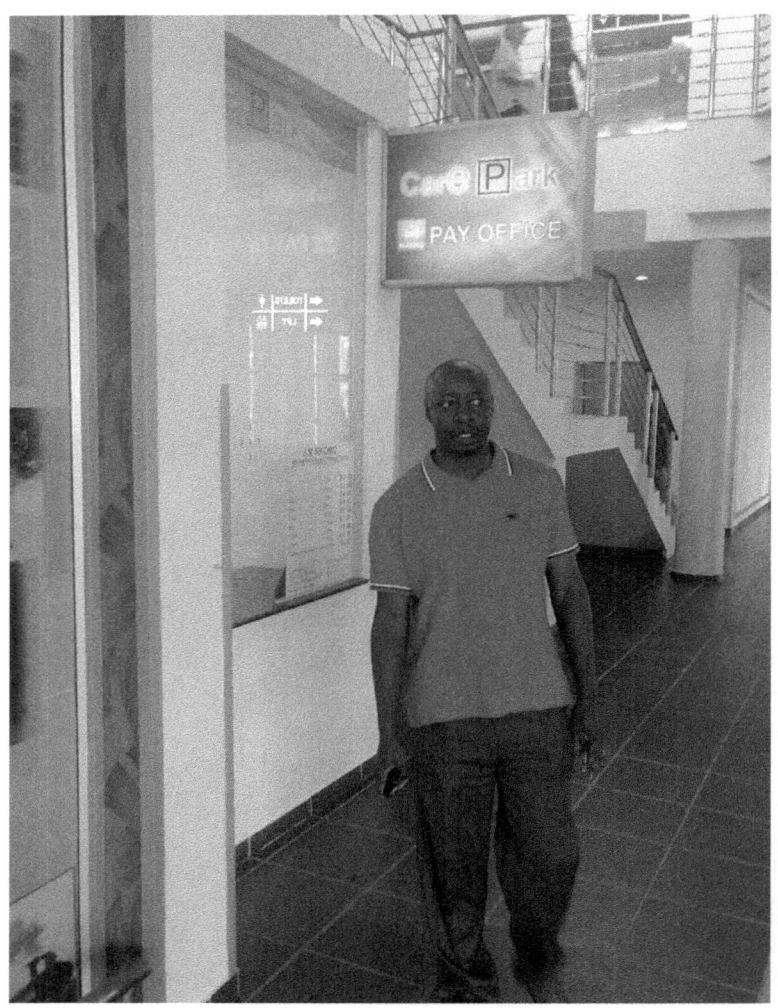

Pentecost Mate is a literary icon of rare fictional attributes. He lives in Bulawayo, Zimbabwe's hub of artistic expression. At 16, he won the first prize in the Randalls National Creative Writing Competition. He was also a first-prize winner in the nation's story reading competition during the launch of *Short Writings from Bulawayo 3*. He is a National Arts Merit Awards nominee. His work has been published in New Delhi, India and in Southern California, USA. He presented a notable academic paper on "Breaking Stereotypes" to international delegates at the ZIBF Indaba Conference. He has more than twenty publications.

A Bright Future for All Humanity

The future of humanity is bright
Like the right amount of light
Beamed from a headlight
Her spirit soars as a plane in flight
Her husband is her new knight
She weeps no more as all is right
His lips search hers every night
In a marriage marked with no fright
As husband and wife no longer fight
And neighbours have ceased to spite

My mind's tongue tastes with all its might
Children enjoying flying a new kite
That showcases an end to their plight
As they no longer have to recite
But surf the internet and cite
All scholars invisible and in sight
Making school moments amusingly light
Like a well-deserved chocolate bite
Whose sugar calories are lite

My mind's nose sniffs a sweet fragrance
Breathtaking, buoyant and barefaced
Wafting through corridors of shop floors
A setting where work is secondary . . .
Human resource satiation is the aspiration
Workers lively mingling from all walks of life
Snacking and licking lips at sit-downs
With high tea mugs and muffins in hand,
Cupful of Cappuccino, crust and queen cakes
Lunch plates spewing with spaghetti and salads,
Grilled chicken cutlets and chili sauced beefsteak

My mind's eye envisions a serene season ahead
Employees certain of their future in companies
Well remunerated and merry
Pleasantly confident of retirement packages
Bonuses paid monthly: workers awash with cash

The Conscious Poets

Brimming away from homes on weekends
In races to keep their bank accounts exhaling

My mind's walking stick feels no obstacles
As streets are free of vendors
All humanity sheltered, fed and clothed
All natural disasters brought on halt
And promoted to new positive positions
Earthquakes shaking baby's rattles to shush them
Volcanos providing thermal energy to industries
Hurricanes vacuum cleaning the emitted gases
Veld fires welding the ozone hole
Epidemics elevated to fast channels of communication
To spread the gospel of good human attributes
And make them pandemic to every living being
Thus, nurturing an indelible fiber of humanity

My mind's touch feels no coldness
When it gropes around pavements
Nations have nourished them with carpets
To cushion the fragile feet of the elderly
Whose numbers have since escalated
As graves have gifted them with long life

An artist's brush paints a colourful universe
A world where continental ideologies merge
Fusing nations' diverse cultural collections,
Weaving them into a bead necklace
That surrounds a single neck . . .
That one world with wide open borders,
That one world with neither visas nor passports
That united world with wide open gates
that allow neighbours' frequent friendly visits
For chats, shared supper and occasional gossip
That one world with one set of feet
To propel it to eternal peace
That one world with one set of arms
To hug each other with love
And embrace our diversity with smiles

The Heart of a Poet

Jyotirmaya Thakur, a retired vice principal, is the author of twenty-one books, an award-winning poet in multiple genres, book reviewer, columnist, editor, literary & social researcher, World Poet Laureate, a living legend of the 21st century, Peace Icon and HPAW Ambassador of Humanity, and Universal Ambassador of Art and Culture of the UNICEF-approved WUAC, Bolivia. Her poems and articles have appeared in more than 200 anthologies in 30 countries, and have been translated into 30 languages. She writes for international magazines, serves on various prestigious committees in many parts of the world, and is a member of numerous associations.

A Glimmer of Hope

When we correspond in peace,
Our minds are at utmost ease,
When we live with gratitude,
We look forward in positive attitude.

Your values are your signature in life,
The jewel box of your soul's insight,
A way of being and a way of life.
The reason of your effortless stride.

Don't look for flaws in any kind,
And even if you find them it is wise,
To be kind and be somewhat blind,
And look for the virtue in any size.

Your values have always been with you.
Build your life around these spilling,
Important things that are good for you,
Clarity and elegance in full abiding.

In pupa stillness we reflect and know,
The blessings as butterflies will flow,
Hands of entropy's great clock shows,
A glimmer of hope that we are not alone.

Trinidadian Brenda Mohammed, poet and writer with a focus on multiple genres, is the recipient of multiple awards. She has twenty-five books to her credit. A former bank manager, Mohammed is an honorary member of the World Higher Literary Academic Council of World Nations Writers Union. In support of new and aspiring authors, she founded "How to Write for Literary Success", a forum which initiated the production of three anthologies, *A Spark of Hope* (2 volumes), *A Treasury of Poems for Saving Lives*, and *Break the Silence: An Anthology Against Domestic Violence*. Each of these publications became an Amazon bestseller.

Hope Beckons

Hope is a shining light that beckons you on.
If you are discouraged and from all, want to run.
When you want to give up and bring it all to an end,
Hope stands tall as your very best friend.

The light at the end of the tunnel keeps glowing.
For the depressed and downtrodden hope keeps flowing.
Whatever the circumstances, where there's life there's hope.
Hope never gives you a chance to sit down and mope.

Hope will show you many things to look forward to.
All you have to do is observe what's around you.
Opportunities abound if you take a real hard look.
You may even get ideas to write a bestselling book.

Each one experiences highs and lows in one's life.
Sometimes we find ourselves amidst terrible strife.
That's no reason to say, 'I can't,' and give up.
Let Hope, Faith, and Love take you to the top.

The Heart of a Poet

Faleeha Hassan, ICPI Cultural Ambassador (Iraq and USA), is a poet, writer, playwright, teacher and an editor. She was born in Iraq and lives in the US. She has an M.A. in Arabic literature and is the first Iraqi woman to write poetry for children. She has 24 books to her credit. Her poems have been translated into many languages, including English, Turkmen, French, Italian, German, Kurdish, and Spanish. Faleeha received many awards in Iraq and throughout the Middle East for her poetry and short stories. She was a 2018 Pulitzer Prize for Poetry and 2019 Pushcart Prize nominee.

If I Didn't Love You, Would I Survive?

Regardless of the fact that I will die like everything on this Earth
And my body will become a fertilizer for the trees
Or
Some of it will stick in the tires of cars
Or
Maybe hungry birds will crave pieces of meat and attack my body with their beaks
I will become an abandoned rubble
Brooms will kick me from one garbage can to another
I say:
Despite all the bad thoughts that may grow in my head
If I didn't love you, would I survive?

The Heart of a Poet

Iwu Jeff (Iwuchukwu Jephta) is a Nigerian creative writer, and instructor of English and literature. His literary work has appeared in many online magazines and anthologies, including Inner Child Press International. A few of his writings have also garnered awards. He is the author of a novel, *Files of the Heart*. His play, *The Verdict of the Gods* is forthcoming.

All Will Be Fine Again

When the night comes – goosy,
with sackcloth longer than a century,
roving & rumbling like tornadoes,
take your eyes off its ticking clock
& your ears off its chattering.

When it becomes a fighting monster,
its claws ripping off your skin,
be not fainted, though it jubilates,
giving you a basketful of lemons,
sip & sip its tangy juices for there lies
the healing for your wounded soul.

Watch & be not a crying tot,
lift up your head & behold the night dissolving
like melted ice at the arrival of the sun, breaking
forth clouds at dawn with rays of hope & laughter.

The Heart of a Poet

Born in Jerusalem, Israel, Tali Cohen Shabtai is a poet. She began writing poetry at the age of six, and she had been an excellent student of literature since. Her early writings on her impressions were published in her school's newspaper. Tali has three poetry books to her credit, *Purple Diluted in a Black's Thick* (bilingual, 2007), *Protest* (bilingual, 2012) and *Nine Years Away from You* (2018). Later in 2020, her fourth collection of poems will be published in Norway. Her literary work has been translated into many languages.

Sisters' Love

Immortality witness
For us.
Stored up in the heart of heaven forever
What was between
Us two.

A refined connection, purified
Of all harm
Looks out from the photographs.

Though our lives are portioned
To pieces of time,
Our existence is eternalized between
The volumes of diaries.

Anwer Ghani, born in 1973 in Babylon, is a 2019 Pushcart nominee, an award-winning poet, a religious scholar and a nephrologist consultant. He has more than a hundred books to his credit. Thirty of them have been published in English, including *A Farmer's Chant* (Inner Child Press International, 2019) and *Warm Moments* (Just Fiction, 2020). Anwer is the editor-in- chief of the Arcs Prose Poetry magazine.

amazon.com/author/anwerghani

The Gaze of the Sea

The sea has a legendary story that penetrates our depths with its stormy love. It paints our world with its unique flavor, and gives life its pungent taste. Its gaze steals the hearts that yearn for it, so they swing like the ships that the waves take away. The sea is our wavy essence, and its wind is a free woman with a charming blue robe. The sea is very soft, but it is violent and leaves no story for the trees, but as you see I sit behind these trees to see the glory of the sea, and melt in my wavy words: "Everything has a rebellious spirit, even you, even me."

Florin M. Ciocea was born in 1957 in Romania.

No Title

Bury your palms in my soul
And bring in light my love for you;
If you don't
The stars will shine less,
And the clear vacuum will fill
With that despair of matter,
Which puts fear in the face of women.

Hide in the deep well of my eyes
To see how much I love the grass,
Forests, mountains and people
And may,
Sometime,
You will love me so much.

If you meet me . . . do not bypass me;
May be season that heals you from sadness,
Or the first snow shivering your cheeks in December.

The Heart of a Poet

Debbi Brody is an avid attendee and leader of poetry workshops throughout the Southwest. Her work has appeared in numerous international, national and regional journals, magazines and anthologies of note. Her newest full-length poetry book is titled *In Everything, Birds* (2015) and her recent chapbook has the title of *Walking the Arroyo*.

artqueen58@aol.com

Wish Fulfillment

I wished for coyote
And she appeared sauntering down a deer path,

I wished for hawk
And saw osprey, kestrel and red tail,

I wished for antelope
And saw two small herds,

I wished for Patsy Kline
And the radio played Sweet Dreams of You,

I wished for home
And we arrived before sunset,

I wished for ease and clarity,
Defragmented my mind and found them.

I wished for a map of love
And you lay down beside me.

Setaluri Padmavathi, a postgraduate in English Literature with a B. Ed., has over three decades of experience in the field of education. During her professional career, she held various positions, such as Head of the Department of English, Academic Coordinator, Principal and teacher. Writing has always been her passion, which translates itself into poems of different genres, short stories and articles on a variety of themes and topics. Padmavathi's poems and other writings regularly appear on Muse India.com, Boloji.com, Science Shore, Setu, and Poemhunter.com.

setaluripadma.wordpress.com

Hope

These saddened days may turn into good days soon
The dark period would pass like a passing cloud
Let's hope for a better morrow, with positive thoughts
We'd fly high like free winged and chirping birds!

We waged the dreadful wars and had seen great loss
We overcame Spanish flew, cyclones, and storms
We're fingers crossed for a new medical discovery
Let's pray for the global health, peace and happiness!

Fear not like a trembling water bird, you're brave!
Worry not for changing times, they bring solace too,
Don't be panic for today, you'd see a better morrow
Come on! Cheer up! The shadowy world would see glow!

You would join your hands with the moving humanity
You'll be the part and parcel of every action of society
You would also cherish the fruitful life and happy days
These tough times will pass like the moving clouds!

All barren lands would certainly turn into farmlands
All enthusiastic men would busily work in firms
All means of transport will soon open new avenues
Let's use the earthly possessions to develop ourselves!

Let's go hand in hand to be more productive than before
Let's build our nation in each and every nook and corner
We, as capable human beings, see the bright side of life
and eliminate the darkness from this beautiful world!

The Heart of a Poet

Padmaja Iyengar-Paddy, former banker and urban governance consultant, is a full-time poet, writer, editor and reviewer. India Book of Records has recognized her maiden poetry collection, *P-En-Chants* as a Unique Record of Excellence. She has compiled the widely-acknowledged international multilingual poetry anthology series *Amaravati Poetic Prism* from 2015 to 2019. Limca Book of Records distinguished this publication as the "Poetry Anthology in Most Languages", with the latest showcasing of 1303 poems in 125 languages by over 761 poets from 86 countries. Paddy is a recipient of several awards and accolades for her contributions and service to literature and poetry.

Hope

Silence all around,
But for an occasional
Coo-hoo of the koel
Or chirping of a sparrow.

This nation-wide lockdown
Seems like a mental break-down
With emptiness staring at me
And hope leaving me . . .

A few stray dogs on my street
eagerly scour for something to eat
I throw some biscuits from my window
And they gratefully accept the treat . . .

I look at the park across my window,
It's been locked down for so long now . . .
I see some flowers withered and
Some leaves turning pale
to soon turn into yellow . . .

Will all the flowers wither off . . .?
Will all the leaves turn yellow . . .?
Was the koel's coo-hoo a plea
To set this world free . . .?

Just as I started losing hope,
Just as I felt I could no longer cope,
I saw clouds gathering in the sky…
Holding out hope and standing by
to provide much needed relief
To this parched earth in grief . . .

They were not clouds foreboding doom
They were not clouds foreboding gloom
They poured down for the flowers to bloom
They poured down to nourish earth's womb.

The Heart of a Poet

Dr. Santosh Bakaya is an academic, a poet, essayist, novelist, biographer, TED-Speaker and creative writing mentor. She has been critically acclaimed for her poetic biography of Mahatma Gandhi, *The Ballad of Bapu*. Her TED-talk on the myth of the writer's block is very popular in the creative writing circles. *Only in Darkness Can You See the Stars* (a biography of Martin Luther King, Jr.) and *Songs of Belligerence* (poetry) are her latest books. Dr. Bakaya runs a well-liked column at Morning Meanderings in Learning and Creativity.com.

Hope Throbs

"Hope is a thing with feathers",
Emily Dickinson had famously said,
and my hope is that that feathered thing
trills from every bough,
every tree, every window sill,
singing songs of hope,
killing all notes of negativity.

Lending my voice to the birds,
I pray that the weak, the meek, the vulnerable
and the destitute will rise.
will rise,
with a love absolute,
hold hands with a tenacity strong,
walk hand in hand and nothing will go wrong
nothing will go wrong
when they rise
with a love absolute,
the borders will fall, the bigots will fall,
the homeless will get homes,
the migrants will no longer be dislodged,
but will snugly lodge in cozy lodges.
I hope on.

As I hope on, a sizzling aroma of delicacies
from mom's kitchen miraculously wafts across to me
from an era gone- the lyrical refrain of a time bygone,
and I am whole once again.

Through my meshed window,
I see dainty, colorful butterflies flitting around,
ears riveted to the music emanating from their wings.
Soon, every breath becomes a silent prayer of
fragile strength.
Hope throbs, resiliently clinging to every dust mote.

The Heart of a Poet

B. S. Tyagi is from India and writes in both Hindi and English. He has several books to his credit – fiction and non-fiction. In addition to his own writings, he has translated four books of poetry. His own poems have been included in several anthologies. He writes short stories which regularly appear in national and international literary magazines. His write-ups and poems have been published in numerous national and international magazines. He shies away from public celebrations and prizes. He views the inner-bliss he is showered upon through creativity as the greatest prize.

Beauty Lies in the Soul

(1)

Only those who're truly blest
With a pure and pristine soul,
Can really praise beauty best,
And ushered into joyous goal,
Save it, nothing is there at all.

(2)

Winter- snow on the tree-tops
And crisp flakes on the still lake,
Urge a man to move with hopes,
Then pious joy knows no brake,
Deep sense of divinity they make.

(3)

Having its feel in depth of soul
Is lighting a lamp in dark room,
And one can hear an inner toll,
That leads away from the doom.
Staying still brings many a bloom.

(4)

If it throws one into restiveness
Then, not worth chasing at all -
If it gives that inner festiveness,
Ever enjoying sans wither or fall,
Attuned to nature to hear its call.

(5)

Beauty without truth is barren land
Where longing dreams never grow,
Fragrance of truth makes it grand –
It shines eternally, but not for show,
Through the soul waters of truth flow.

(6)

Truth makes the sun shine within soul
That dispels darkness growing for ages,
And he regains the state before the Fall,
Mortal frame lastly falls to times' rages.

Rahim Karim (Karimov), poet, writer, publicist and translator of Uzbek, Russian, Kyrgyz and Soviet origin, is a graduate of the M. Gorky Moscow Literary Institute. He is a member of the National Union of Writers of the Kyrgyz Republic, the Union of Writers of Russia and Belgium's International Writers Association; a London and Budapest-representative of the International Federation of Russian-Speaking Writers in Kyrgyzstan, and laureate of Moldo Niyaz and Egemberdi Ermatov literary prizes. He has an Honorary Ph.D. from Morocco, is co-chair of the Literature Council of the Eurasian Peoples' Assembly, and laureate of the International Peter Bogdani Prize.

Hope

A wick burns in my heart, whose name is Hope,
A candle is burning in my heart called Hope.
In my heart there is a light bulb called Hope,
A fire burns in my heart that bears the name Hope.

The sun shines in my heart, the so-called Hope,
Love burns in my heart, which strives for Life.
Vera burns in my heart that she believes in a brighter future
A fire called Hope will not go out in my heart.

Faith in God Almighty burns in my heart,
Faith in the future of Humanity burns in my heart.

For the past 30 years, Dr. Ashok Chakravarthy Tholana has been persistently composing message-oriented poetry to promote universal peace, world brotherhood, environmental consciousness, nature protection, safeguarding of children's and human rights, uplifting the downtrodden, etc. His articles on human rights and universal peace have been highly praised. During his 30-year stint with poetry, his work acquired a rare distinction of getting published in no less than 90 countries, and he had the privilege of being conferred with several prestigious national and international awards, laurels, commendations, citations and titles. Out of his 18 volumes of English poetry, 7 have been published so far.

http://peacefromharmony.org/?cat=en_c&key=286
https://www.youtube.com/channel/UC6_potXgqfRLXr5GDkegQiQ

Offering Love and Solace

The heart of a poet, is calm and composing
Aspires to peep into the hearts of suffering;
With a hope to pacify with words and actions
A poet thirsts to perform like a moral human.

Upholding human values with a righteous spirit
Uplifting the sagging morale of the deprived lot;
A poet seeks to bring to light the hidden truths
Devoid of bias, irrespective of religions and faiths.

Vying to promote a healthy and cordial relation
Poets jot verses to boost the human compassion,
Yes, striving for a better future for all of humanity
They weave words of trust, concern and humility.

Realize! Moral actions reflect a life's real essence
Let not our ignorance snatch away life's fragrance;
Perhaps the heart of every poet follows the concept
Offering love and solace with an unwavering precept.

Sujata Dash is a poet from Bhubaneswar, Odisha. She is a retired banker. She has a poetry anthology, *More Than a Mere Bunch of Poems* to her credit. She is a singer and an avid lover of nature. She regularly contributes to anthologies worldwide with her poems.

All Is Not Lost

All is not lost
only our faith and belief are put to toss
this too will pass this too will go
the forward is taking baby steps
the process remains a bit slow
we need not lose heart
for . . . we have begun anew painting life's canvas
the desert will flourish . . . hope will fruition to oasis
wishes will bloom desire will blossom
we can brave it and wipe out from horizon

The pandemic has taken its toll
yet remains unstoppable, is on a roll
the scare has crippled mind and core
fear of losing near and dear ones
has shrouded the entire atmosphere
on this backdrop we need to act strong
consolidate for a better future
the scare will be part of our life for sometime
we are to evolve in respect of habits and perspective
hold hands and stand by each other like tower
for it remains need of the hour

We have faced many misfortunes
countered many onslaughts
yet, each time emerged victorious
there will be turn around for sure
with patience and fine tuning, we shall better our score
absolute intent never fails nor fervent hope disappoints
soon, we shall be on winning spree indulge in mirth, happiness
pulsating, riveting clicks will simmer with life's essence.

Thryaksha A. Garla has been writing since she was a little kid. She has a blog and an Instagram account with about 250 poems posted to this date. She touches upon themes such as feminism, self-reliance, love, but she mostly writes blues. Her poems have been published in two issues of the *Sparks* magazine, and in poetry anthologies, such as *Efflorescence of Chennai Poets' Circle, The Current, The Metverse Muse, Our Poetry Archive, Destine Literare, Untamed Thrills and Shrills, Float Poetry,* and in the Setu e-magazine.

@thryaksha_wordsmith
https://thryaksha.wordpress.com/

Tomorrow Is Always Brighter

You've been through a lot,
You've given everyone so much,
You've sacrificed,
But give yourself some time.
You've thought of them all,
You've messed up,
You've made mistakes,
But come out of it.
You've gone low,
You've given up,
You've faulted yourself,
But now move on.
Leave the past,
Say goodbye,
Flash forward,
Look in front.
There's happiness,
Waiting to shine,
As long as you decide,
To do it now.

Khalid Imam, a bilingual Nigerian poet, writer, playwright, teacher, translator, editor and reviewer, coordinates the All Poets Network. In 2017, he was selected by the Wole Soyinka Foundation to participate in SAIL. He served as the Vice Chairman of the Association of Nigerian Authors in the Kano State branch. He has received multiple awards and has published in the US, Canada, India, Germany and Poland. Among other books, he has authored *A Song of San Kano* (2010), *Sodangi* (2010), *The Amigo Sisters* (2016), *Barde Barbushe* (2017), and *Falsafar Bukar Usman* (2019).

Hope and Hoping

Nothing else
keeps life sweet and
amazing like the alluring smile of hope –
reassuring us all is well at life's riverside.

There,
like the cheerful spouse on honeymoon
the birds should always play hide-and-seek unmolested,
daring the monstrous eyes of the menacing wavy tides
engorging the canoes of our dreams.

What else is hope if not that
freshly flowing river, the merry birds
mate, bathe and fish in.

What else
throws its embracing arms wide
to save us from our dreadful daily despair
and depression than hope and hoping.

True, the riverside
is an optimistic buddy
all wise ones frequent -
to listen to its dovish voice whispering calmly:
take my hands hey you pal
to be thrilled by the gentle wind
and the cuddle of fresh air only hope offers.

What else if not hope spurs
a toddler to persistently
keep rising after many falls.

What else reconciles estranged
lovers to embrace again and again
if not hope and hoping!

Suma K. Gopal fell in love with poetry as a child. Her poems, written through inevitable moments of change, are quiet expressions that help her unmask. She hails from a small village in Kerala, India, and writes in English and Malayalam. Her poetry has appeared in various international anthologies. Suma is a trained Carnatic classical singer and a senior Human Resources professional in a multinational organization based in Bangalore.

The Deluge

Indeed, it was unbearably hot
Hawks yearned looking up
For soothing drops of rain
To sate the parched barren land

Murky clouds loomed up
Into hazy portentous shapes
Threatening a frenzy eruption
Drowning everything in nothingness

Maybe it's the end of melodrama
The deluge may wash away the banal earth
Its distortions and despair
And green thoughts sprout with newer roots.

*At an underlying level, the poem attempts to capture what it feels like when one goes through an episode of depression. It explores a range of experiences and some of the complex feelings during the bouts, but ends with hope, healing and evolution.

Menduh Leka, a writer from Kosovo, is poet and editor of mearteka.com. He has published over 10 books of poetry, various studies, etc. His poems have appeared in English, Italian and Croatian anthologies, including *The Muse*, the contemporary editions of *Amazona*, *Prosopisia* and *Diogen*.

Take Care of the Harmony of Echoes

They have the right to play hand in hand
to dance to the rhythm of the breeze with no contaminated taste
Give them the divine right not to hear the noise of grenades or COVID-19
when they fall down and break the smiling faces
Little serenity until they paint dreams
Did you ever follow
erratic flight of a butterfly when automatic rifle strikes
Or did you ever observe the sun when the smokescreen cover viewing
when blown up with dynamite then flesh and iron and souls disappear?
You would do well to slow down the pace.
Take some of their time
Take care of God's desire
And the harmony of echoes
Horror will not last forever
But music and peace
When you armor someone's love and your day ends
you lie on the corpses for a nap
with hundreds of consecutive questions
that come to your mind?
You would do well to slow down breathing and pace.
life has the advantage so please do not destroy it so quickly.
Time don't exist, mind energy is Essence
Only the music lasts forever.
And the harmony of echoes for peace around the globe.
And you who fire on a flower or a bird or a man or a butterfly
have you ever heard the music of life?
Do not rush because you have forgotten to take away the voice of peace
Here should remain the Planet of Peace
And climb somewhere to the Dark Planet and dance the deaths' dances
In that planetary madhouse far away from souls that dance
Hand in hand and smile to the God and Freedom
Allow them to enjoy and live in Peace Planet
In the harmony with all echoes.
With music that will definitely live forever.

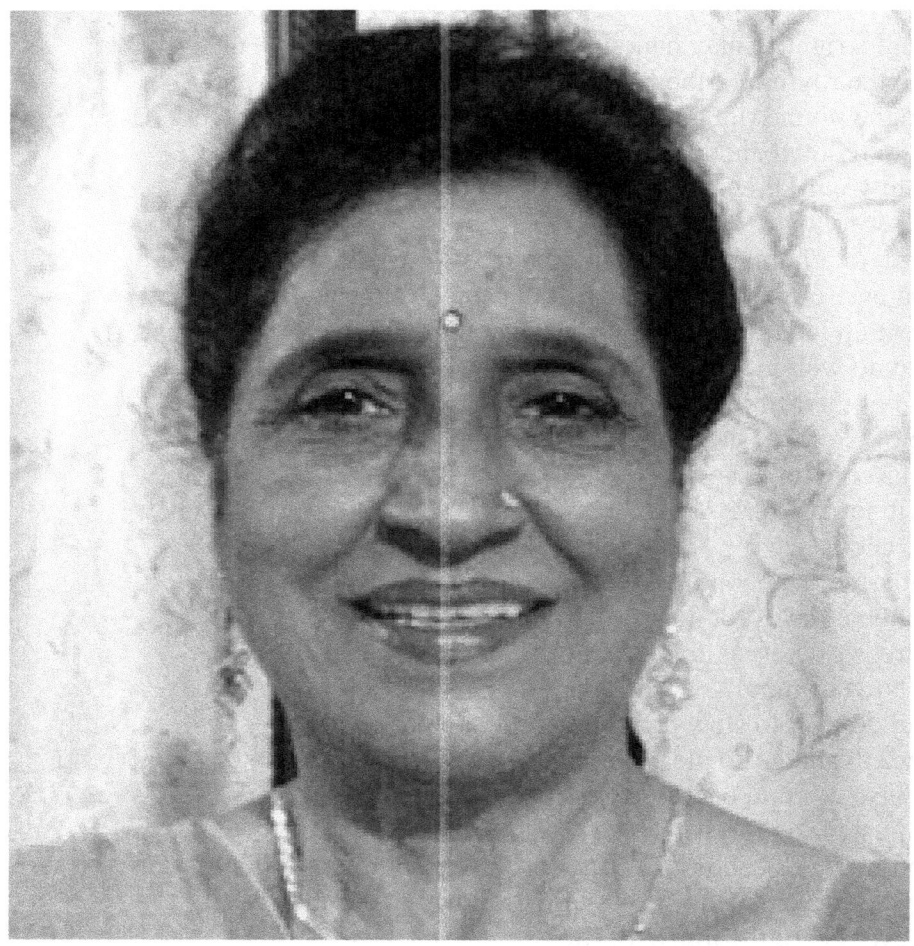

Pushmaotee Subrun studied at Delhi University and worked in Zimbabwe and Mauritius. A member of the Council of the University of Mauritius, she is currently an editor in the Ministry. She authored *Ella, Who Is Your Best Friend?* and *Short Stories and Fables. Dreams to Reality*. Her new book, *A Lyrical Bouquet of Soulful Poems* is pending publication. Her poems appeared in prestigious e-zines and anthologies, including Setu, Atunis Galaxy Anthology, OPA Anthology of Poetry, *Amaravati Poetic Prism, Inner Child Press International*, Best Poetry, and Destiny Poets where she was selected Poet of the Year and Critic of the ICOP 2019 awards.

Hope, the Universal Panacea

Hope is what has always sustained humanity,
Why not hope for a better day in unanimity?
When our natural world has revived,
The smog over Los Angeles has cleared,
The snow-capped Himalayas have cleared its mists,
The earth's upper crust has calmed according to seismologists.
All wonderful reminders that nothing lasts forever,
Undoubtedly, the pandemic will not last forever.
The world is threatened with the domino effect ominously,
Bankruptcies, unemployment and Chinese Whispers, portentously.
But what we need is dose of optimism imminently.

We might not win immediately
But surely, we shall win ultimately.
Airports are not functioning normally
Due to our health being a priority.
Retailers, casino workers, restaurants, universities,
Factories and all sectors will soon be like busy bees.
The media is spreading news of recession
Or a collapse of our society with depression,
And food shortages or other ticking time bombs.
Discouraging news to lead us earlier to our tombs!
Best is to boost our moral strength with encouraging aplomb!

Replenishing the self is more than vital,
Nurturing our inner world for better survival,
What with continuous challenges, revitalizing our batteries,
It's crucial to reconnect with those elevating galaxies,
And do something we enjoy deeply, for once,
Like spending quality time in confinement with loved ones,
In vitalizing, refreshing nature walking and breathing,
With ourselves and our environment reconnecting,
For ideally healing, far from morbid thoughts engaging.
With new life in us, we shall definitely get rid of stress
And positive qualities harness.

The Conscious Poets

So, let us steel ourselves mentally, physically,
And spiritually to bounce enthusiastically.
With the key coping mechanism
Of using valuable time to bring new enthusiasm,
Opening the mind to beneficial alternatives
Such as exercising, reading, painting or other derivatives,
Like poetry writing, watching inspiring or comic films or clips,
Going on YouTube for motivational trips,
Calling friends, uplifting their morale, trying new recipes,
Or engaging in sensational potted plants to promote cheerfulness.
For after all, being productive will bring about wellness.

Moreover, with unwavering faith, instill,
The air with fervent thanks and good vibes fill,
For bestowed blessings by the Almighty's Will.
Let hope, prayer and faith illuminate and fulfil,
As they strengthen realism that we can prevail.
Let's confront the brutal facts, and opportunities avail,
Incessantly imploring the Heavens for mercy on us to prevail.
Nothing will our determination mar
If we be in hope as fixed as the Northern Star.
Come thunder, lightning or rain,
However blighted our lot, our stars will shine again!

The Heart of a Poet

Dr. Ranjana Sharan Sinha, a professor of English, poet, writer and critic, is an outstanding voice in Indian Poetry in English. She has received numerous awards for her poems and contributions to literature, including a commendation from the former President of India for her poem "Mother Nature". Two of her poems were included in the English M.A. program. Her poems, short stories, articles and research papers were published widely in print and online. She has 7 published books in different genres and 50 research papers. Currently, she is research supervisor at the RTM Nagpur University in India.

The Wings of Hope

Sometimes, an alien night!
Blues come,
first in a trickle,
then in a flood –
A sea of spiked hyacinths:
Incarcerated sorrows!
But still, like a dolphin,
hope leaps out –
I see a mermaid
emerge from the deep
amid the cursive tides of night:
The aquamarine jewels
with the shimmer of moonlight –
Mystical and magical!

Sometimes, disappointment
on the stony roads –
treeless under a scorching sun,
Bleak like barren-brown deserts,
Ruthless like carnivorous breaths
threatening to swallow!
But still, like a desert flower,
hope dares to blossom!
My mind weaves rainbows
beautiful with seven colours!
On the iridescent wings of hope,
my heart soars high
into a cool cosmos!

Hema Ravi is a freelance trainer for IELTS and Communicative English. Her poetic publications include HAIKU, Tanka, free verse and metrical verses. Her write-ups have been published in *The Hindu*, *New Indian Express*, *Femina*, *Woman's Era* and several online and print journals; a few of her haiku and form poems have been prize-winners. She is the author of *Everyday English, Write Right Handwriting Series 1, 2, 3*, and the co-author of *Sing Along Indian Rhymes* and *Everyday Hindi*.

hemaravi24@gmail.com

Nothing but the Truth

Spell bound, statue like
in the presence of a blooming flower
soaking in the zephyr
while the leaves nod goodbye
as they soar to newer horizons
The clear blue sky gives way
to the dense grey clouds
Swaying - whispers of trees get louder
Petrichor filling the nostrils tingle
Watching the first droplets of water
gentle, at first, then in torrents . . .
The canvas now has changed into meadow green
after the heavenly wash, with splashes of
red, pink, mauve and lavender
against the dazzling brightness
grand finale to the heavenly symphony
The eyes never tire!

The pristine scene torn to shreds
when the eye roves on
to the muck and filth of polluted waters
bloodied with slaughtered beasts and corpses
Debris from human by habitation
The sweat-stained faces of the milieu
Bee-hive of men and women
in high rising edifices
Exacerbating scenes of civilization
fills the chalice that earlier
had ambrosia to the brim . . .
As a seer burst into verse
to curse the hunter aiming
at a pair of birds in conjugal bliss
the poet's empathetic heart mirrors sights
that are joyous, disgusting
exciting, enticing, awe inspiring or horrific
with the awareness that kaleidoscopic
changes go on and on,
the large screen behind remains intact!

The Heart of a Poet

Born in Trois-Rivières – the city currently recognized for poetry, Louise Hudon moved to Abitibi in 1971. For 35 years, she worked for the same employer, the Lac-Abitibi School Board. She enjoyed her vast experiences, especially those with children, at the Academy of Assumption during her teaching year. She obtained her degree in Sciences of Education from the University of Quebec in Rouyn-Noranda, Québec. Published in several world collectives, she has composed four books, three of which are poem collections. She remains very active in her writing endeavors.

They Saw Me

In honour of those who have suffered from depression or still suffer from it to this day

They saw me, ill,
No more laughing,
Only serious, can no longer fool others,
The news is now circulating.

In order to judge, one must know,
Learn from history,
The shocks, the trauma,
All far from romanticism . . .

So many emotions
Attacking and overwhelming!
All these negative emotions
Devastating . . .

I only want to understand,
Without making a scene,
My thoughts are never-ending,
I have to isolate and avoid others.

Please don't judge me
And maybe you will see.
You will finally understand
That I am alone and depressed.

They tell me that with time
And a radiant sun
My body will renew itself
Will learn to finally relax.

Please hope
Distance yourself from the fear
Hold onto it for as long as it takes
With your fighting spirit.

The Heart of a Poet

With your happiness rekindled
Once again motivated
You will once again find your path
All will be well; you will be yourself again.

We wish health to all humanity. Hope is there.

Sameer Goel is a seasoned teacher, human rights activist, journalist and a respected writer. His work appears under his pen name, @iammusaafiir. His passion for writing and the appreciation of his words are evidenced through his noted presence in numerous anthologies, including *Ishq-e-Watan, Clipped Wings Grow, Letters to Self, #metoo, Ala Rasi, Unheard Words of Soul, Miseries of the World, Clipped Wings Glow* and *Color My Dreams*. His debut book, *Ginger Hues, Dripping Honey* is a collection of short quotes and epigrams about the experiences and aspirations we all have from our lives.

I Dream

if i get, ever so lost in my dreams,
i will bring you back all the stars so far . . .
starry notebooks where every dream redeems,
soothing every nerve, healing every scar . . .

illusory dreams, often deceive us,
entice, taking us to the silhouettes . . .
break hearts often, visions magnanimous
if dreamt surreal using old lorgnettes . . .

i, for sure, shall bring back smiles, those blessings,
fill those trenches, those smiles buried deeper . . .
remove the scars, a touch so caressing,
sowing efforts, becoming grand reaper . . .

i just dream all about love, peace and joy
a vison, clearing every mind of coy . . .

From Kokuvil, Sri Lanka, Somasuntharampillai Pathmanthan ('Sopa') is the recipient of several state and provincial awards. He has published 3 volumes of his own poetry and 3 collections of poems in translation. He has also translated Shanmugalingam's plays into English. His work has appeared in prestigious journals abroad. 'Sopa', as he is popularly known in literary circles, has presented papers in many international venues, including the SAARC Literature Festivals (Delhi) and Poets Translating Poets (Frankfurt, Mumbai and Chennai).

The Future Is Ours

We're heirs to great achievers
The giants who built
The great wall of China
The Hanging gardens of Babylon
Mohenjo-Daro and Harappa
The Pyramids of Egypt
Maya and Machu Picchu

No cause for alarm
No need for despair

The last millennium
Saw Franklin and Faraday
Edison and Einstein
Who made our life
Comfortable

Man explored the Cosmos
His giant strides in Communication
Demolished
Barbed wires and boundary walls
And brought nations and peoples
Incredibly closer

Here we stand
On top of the world
On the horizon we see
Buddha and Christ
Gandhi and Mandela
Cautioning the world
Not to go astray

The Conscious Poets

No cause for alarm
No need for despair

Let's forge ahead
The future is ours!

The Heart of a Poet

Zinia Mitra, from Siliguri, Darjeeling, teaches English in the University of North Bengal. Her poems have appeared in national and international journals, including *Muse India, Ruminations, Contemporary Literary Review, Kavya Bharati, East Lit., Indian Literature, Asian Signature, Teesta Review,* and *Setu*. Her translations have been published in books and journals, such as *Indian Literature* and *Sahitya Akademi*. Her books include *Indian Poetry in English: Critical Essays, Poetry of Jayanta Mahapatra: Imagery and Experiential Identity, Twentieth Century British Literature: Reconstructing Literary Sensibility* (co-edited), *Interact* (co-edited) and *The Concept of Motherhood in India: Myths, Theories and Realities*.

About This Rain

No one has written about this rain,
this rain that drenched me
this rain that walked uninvited across my lost-umbrella day
doused the emerald grass, succulent leaves, furrowed barks.
No one has written about these fine gray lines
that trembled at the edge of this autumnal storm
like silver hair on an aging face,
the hushed approval of the last ardent sunrays
the gasping moment before the rain
when the world suspended itself and hung from the sky,
I collect these transient moments
because I write about this rain.

We all perceive when lightning strikes distant lands.

The Heart of a Poet

Kwame MA McPherson, Poetic Soul winner (2007) and Flash Fiction Awardee of The Bridport Prize International Creative Writing Competition (2020), facilitates motivational and creative writing workshops and presentations. His most recent appearance was at the University of Westminster, England. His written work has been endorsed by the University of West Indies and appeared in *The Lime Jewel*, an anthology for the 2010 Haitian Earthquake victims, Frederick_Cooper's award-winning novel *Unbreakable* and international magazines [. . .] His latest book, *My Date with Depression: Mental Uncertainty to Self-Fulfilment* (2019), voices his experience of dealing with depression.

On Whose Shoulders I Stand

I look at my hands
Chapped
I wipe the sweat from my brow
Made from the seeds I need to sow
I feel my muscles scream
Is my life a nightmare, not *the* dream?
I wake everyday
Most times we go hungry
while I struggle to be something
For others to see
To me
To my family
Even to a wider nation
It hurts, yet I must have hope
Since it was who went before, their shoulders I stand
I may not have it today,
I may not have it tomorrow
But they endured so much more
Lifting me up, helping me to soar
They hold my hands
They push me to higher heights
They uplift me when the next step is not in sight
They say it's okay, we have your back, each and every way

The Heart of a Poet

Dr. T. Sree Latha, Head & Associate Professor of Training & Placement Cell at the NRI Institute of Technology in Vijayawada, India, has been teaching for 25 years. She has presented more than 56 research papers at various national and international conferences, and her work has appeared in numerous journals. She believes in eternal learning and therefore attends workshops and seminars. She aims to explore Sri Aurobindo's *Savitri* for her future research articles. Her poems have been published in English and Telugu. Her hobbies include giving verbal form to inner thoughts, listening to classical music and playing Veena.

When Tomorrow Comes

Days of intense slumber and reluctance roll dully
Yearned for days of profuse stir and activity gaily
Brooded on the changes thrust by the obscure hand
Fancied to bring back the cordial days with a wand
Observed life's turns after the hit of the pandemic
Cherished human's support even to outer domestic
Recalled the concept of 'Vasudhaiva Kutumbakam'
That did not allow me waste time and remain numb

Enabled me foresee a better world in all facets fully
Humanity learnt the lessons of carelessness carefully
Realized the need of personal distance once ignored
Valued the customs of other people once abhorred
Ascertained the harm caused by Man to the planet
Discovered the promotion done to Nature's blanket
Wondered at the beauty of mountains now visible
Surprised at the purity of river waters now credible

Learnt to complete official affairs with due respect
Shouldered the nation's economy in every prospect
Honestly volunteered to help and uplift the needy
Inspired others to do the same without being greedy
Admired at the harmony of men in many references
Loved to see the humanity work beyond differences
Many turned up to see themselves as self-made men
As 'Necessity is the mother of invention,' since then

Respected the lives of the life giving disaster managers
Saluted those lives survived against high risk damagers
Prayed for the families of those fighting for taut security
Called upon the Almighty to relieve them from that duty
Knelt down for a quick cure to the world's start afresh
It is HE who rescues the mankind with a heart of flesh
Believed that people overcome pain and definitely gain
It is the eternal record recorded by them time and again.

Akshaya Kumar Das has authored and published a collection of English poems, *The Dew Drops*, and made numerous contributions to various international & Indian anthologies with his poetry. He is the recipient of numerous international awards, including the Ambassador of Humanity Award from Ghana. In 2017, Das organized an International Poetry Festival under the aegis of Feelings International Artists Society in Bhubaneswar, India. He is an administrator & analyst for the Poemariam Poetry Group. He was a featured poet for the Pentasi B. Poetry Group. He resides in Bhubaneswar, India.

The Dreams of a Poet

Dreams of a poet,
To serve the vast humanity,
Educate & emancipate poverty,
Any form of insanity . . .
Food, water & shelter,
Basic needs of men, women & children
Need special attention
Appeal to the rich & well-to-do,
To serve the vast humanity,
To narrow the vast gap,
The vast gap between rich & poor,
Divides the humanity,
In the name of caste, creed, race & colour,
The different countries face the poor,
See the vast multitude suffer,
While few relish with opulence,
The vast majority struggles to eke out a living,
When this vast gap narrows down,
Shall benefit millions of hungry men, women & children,
It may be a poetic dream,
That one day equality will reign in the world,
Every man & woman get their due share of the cake to be shared,
A wake-up call to the rich,
What will you do with so much wealth?
Can't you see the poor struggling for health,
When millions just starve without food, water & a roof,
Why don't you volunteer & come forward,
To share the pain & pleasure of the starved world?

The Heart of a Poet

Rita Stanzione was born in Salerno, Italy where she lives to date. After she completed her studies in pedagogy, she taught scientific subjects, and later, specialized in teaching for disabled children. She writes poems regularly – in HAIKU-form or otherwise, and is an accomplished translator (English language-poetry into Italian). She began to publish her poetic work in 2012. As of 2017, her publications include *Canti di carta*, *Di ogni sfumatura*, and *Grammi di ciglia e luminescenze, 60 Haiku*. Her poems have appeared on Italian and international websites. She has received numerous prizes in poetry competitions throughout Italy.

She Moves
Dedicated to Flora, the goddess of the blooms of ancient Rome

She moves
the trembling ribbon
of joy
the foot of the wave
that carries sky blue
toward purple

Flora dances
the fleeing moments
the elusive heart
of a smiling age
a legend that belongs
to the summer

Translated by Ute Margaret Saine

'Siv' is a bilingual poet, published author, short story writer, novelist, translator and an essayist. His novel, *On the Banks of a River* is in English. He has participated in several international poetry festivals where he presented his poems. In 2017, he won the prestigious Ampasayya Naveen Literary Trust's Award for *Harivillu*, his maiden Telugu novel. In 2018, he was distinguished as the ninth prize-winner in the International English Short Story Competition conducted for the 4th Bharat Award. He has three books in Telugu – a collection of short stories, a poetry collection and a collection of translated stories.

Surging Ahead

Despite the pandemics, obstacles
Viruses, unforeseen catastrophes
And other numerous natural calamities
This far has come the human race
Night dies and delivers the day
Day takes a sojourn to make
The universe falls asleep
As a mother holds her babies
The heaven carries the rain bearing clouds
And soothes the parched earth
With its seasonal showers
Moon lights the land and stars
With a silver tint
Which is as pure as its heart
When man faults
The nature corrects
His myriad mistakes
With an undying hope
That his tolerance for the other
Creatures, beings, religions, faiths
And innumerable entities
Unconditionally grows
For hope is the engine
That drives the mankind
Eternally forward!!!

The Heart of a Poet

Avijit Roy was born in West Bengal, India in 1985. He earned his degree in English Literature from Calcutta University in 2006. At present, he is a teacher in a high school in his native state. His first published book is *Sela, the River Princess* (2019). His other books are *Children of a Whimsical God*, *A Late Sunrise*, *Pictorial Biography of William Shakespeare*, *A Return Gift for Santa* and *Wings of Dreams*. His stories have been published in international magazines, including *WINK, Pangolin Review, Breaking Rule Publisher*, and *Brilliant Flash Fiction*.

A New Dawn

As I stood at the lonely window and saw
The lanes below glistened like snake scales.
The skeletal houses held their breath,
As the silent hearse chanted Death's hymns.
A sudden cacophony shattered the awe
When a peacock descended
On the concrete breast of the city
Bled by the claws of miniature plague.
Fearless the bird drunk in nectar,
Poured the divine bliss in somnolent eyes.
My soul danced with his marvelous wings,
That he spread like an aura of salvation.
The world will rise up from her sick bed,
And look straight at the rising sun.
One day the lonely streets will vibrate,
With human souls fluttering in heavenly dance.

The Heart of a Poet

Born in 2002, Sahaj Sabharwal loves writing poems and thoughts. He lives in Jammu city in the Indian union territory of Jammu and Kashmir. He has a published book, *Poems by Sahaj Sabharwal*, and received many poetry awards at state, national and international levels. He was an invitee to the International Writers Meeting in Tarija and Hungary and was recognized with the International Diploma in Writing and International Merit Certificate in Writing. His work was published by The Young Writers Association in UK, for which he received a certificate of publication. Sabharwal has also received the India Star Proud Award.

Hope Never Results in a "Nope"

Hope our eyes will never tell a lie,
And our confidence level will never die.

Hope the forests will always remain clean and green,
And the earth will enjoy this frabjous scene.

Hope our good dreams will come true,
And nobody in this planet will rue.

Hope the sun always keep shining,
And for UV Protection, ozone will always form a thick lining.

Hope everyone lives in peace and harmony,
And no one will perform any illegal activity for more money.

Hope all humans will perform their assigned passionate roles,
And everyone reaches their desired goals.

But most important thing is to keep scope of hope,
Which will never result in a "nope".

Dilip Mohapatra (b. 1950), a decorated Navy Veteran from Pune, India is a highly acclaimed poet in contemporary English. His poems appeared in many literary journals of repute and multiple anthologies worldwide. He has six poetry collections in English to his credit so far, published by Authors Press, India. He is the recipient of many awards and honours in India and abroad.

dilipmohapatra.com

Picking up the Pieces

Even before the tectonic tremors
have made a full retreat
leaving deaths and devastations
in their wake
a broken and bloodied
forearm sticking
out of the rubbles here
the decapitated head
of a marble Buddha rolling out there
a little boy crying for help
deep down the crevice
that runs like a black serpent
along the caved in tarred road
torn and mangled corrugated sheets
strewn around amidst
the debris of twisted rods
broken bricks and splintered
wooden boards
the old monk in his
tattered ochre robe
looks around for the lost
brass bell that has been
ripped off the temple tower
so that he may
reinstall it once again
for it to ring once again
ushering in new hopes
new aspirations
and a new beginning . . .

Bhisma Upreti is an award-winning Nepali poet and writer. He has published 9 poetry books, 9 books of essays / travel notes, and one novel. He is the recipient of the SAARC Literature Award along with numerous other awards. His literary work has been translated into English, Hindi, Sinhala, Russian, Cambodian, Serbian, Slovenian, Macedonian, Japanese, Korean and Bangla, and has appeared in many books, anthologies and literary journals. He is a secretary of PEN Nepal (Nepalese Center of PEN International). He lives in Kathmandu with his family.

bhisma.upreti@gmail.com

The Light of Hope

Burning severely this intense dissatisfaction
and right through its billowing thick smoke
Signing the dreams out that are clear/unclear
all over the road
and flowing over it, covering its both edges
a procession has just left from here.

As the procession left
along with the anarchism
it also has dropped
some portions of hope.
Along with vulgarity and toadyism
it has also dropped bunches of dawn-hope.

Clearing the footsteps left by the procession
Now some children have come out to the road
and gathering there
they are carrying some amount of light
dropped by the procession.
They are playing with the bunches of hope
dropped by the procession.

I, about to be swallowed by the time
am sure about the civilized tomorrow of the people.
This is not because of the procession
that had walked along this way, but the children
carrying the same lights of hope
on the road.

Translated by Pancha Vishmrit

The Heart of a Poet

Born in 1970 in India, Otteri Selvakumar is an Alternative Physician who has a Ph.D. in Yoga. His favorite undertakings are writing poetry, making love, photography, dancing, writing, and singing hip hop, alternate rap and pop songs. He has seven published poetry books in English and in 40 other languages. He has translated and published HAIKU poems in more than 40 world tongues. Over 10,000 poems of his appeared on various websites. He describes his dream as follows: "To write better tomorrow than today."

otteriselvakumar@gmail.com

The Life of Reality

Get down there
The leaves fall off
Looking at the sky
Laughing
That tree . . .
Please don't cut it
The reason is . . .
That tree today
The age will be 300
You can . . . not live that long

I know
And you know that . . .
But . . . that tree doesn't know

That's the tree of hope
Not just identity
Today's life . . . today
Crop of Shadow . . . Yesterday

A resident of Quirino, Isabela, Jodel E. Agbayani has graduated in 2014 with a B.A. in Secondary Education, majoring in English at the Isabela State University. He has been publishing his work on different platforms, including NoInk ABS-CBN Publishing and Asia-Pacific Consortium of Researchers and Educators. At present, he is a Senior High School Teacher at Quirino National High School. He has held this position for three fruitful years, while he continues to study toward his doctoral degree in Education in the Echague campus of the Isabela State University.

What Hope Awaits

Just a simple, plain and monotonous
Variants of being credulous
Time beats as fast as human hearts
Always, as if usual, changes so hard

Looking at things differently
Could really make you feel extraordinary
Perceiving the beauty of things, it radiates
Brings a total glance of many that still awaits

Embrace mine, embrace yours
Hold tight, fight until it will be yours
Accentuate GOD's faithfulness
Surely, His love fosters you with joyfulness

Dare to believe, to act and to hope
For success sewed in your own personal rope
Embrace your dreams!
That's the power of a great dreamer who dreams!

The Heart of a Poet

Shareef Abdur-Rasheed, "Zakir Flo" as his spiritual expression, was born and raised in Brooklyn, New York. He completed his education in Brooklyn College, Suffolk County Community College and Makkah, Saudi Arabia. He is a Vietnam-era veteran. In 1969, Shareef reverted to his now reverently embraced Islamic faith. He is highly active in the Islamic community and beyond with his teachings, activism and humanity. Never silent, Shareef always drops science, love, consciousness and signs of the time in rhyme. He is the patriarch of the Abdur-Rasheed family with 9 children (6 sons, 3 daughters) and 41 grandchildren (24 boys, 17 girls).

https://www.facebook.com/shareef.abdurrasheed1

https://zakirflo.wordpress.com

Magnificent

relevance magnitude
of mercy
extended to helpless
souls of destiny
ease will overcome
difficulty
scale will shift
pendulum swing
that which life brings
patience, prayer, trust
remains . . .
formula
promised by most high
after every period of difficulty
there is ease
twice as much ease
remember!
we're here to be tested
not chill everlasting rested
not here
but wait, promised to come
my dear
to those with god fear
persevere!
one cannot just boost trust
mantle will be tested in us
thus dem who exude patience
prayer
persevere!
dem who trust in most merciful
persevere!
those who believe will see
twice as much ease win over
difficulty
keep the faith y'all, please!

From Poland, Lilla Latus is a poet, translator, reviewer, song lyrics and travel articles writer. She has been recognized with numerous awards for her poems and engagement in cultural activities for local communities. She has published nine poetry books. Her poems have also appeared in many journals and anthologies in Poland and abroad.

Hope

tiny and fragile

like a soldier's
dog tag
or an old
black and white
photograph

enduring and hard

like family house
walls

never ready to die

collapsing on demand

The Heart of a Poet

Umasree Raghunath, Senior IT Professional with IBM, is an author, blogger, poet, lawyer, Diversity & Inclusion Social Activist, motivational speaker, the past president of Inner Wheel Club of Madras South, and vice president of eWIT. Umasree has been writing poetry since the age of 13, and has around 400 poems of various themes, subjects, situations and emotions to her credit.

Light the Candle of Hope

The world is gripping with death & fear
War with the infinitesimal enemy near
Time to raise with faith and not fear
Sadness, hopelessness and several unshed tears

Looking into the eye of the storm
and time to remain resilient and calm
Lord, what are you wanting us to learn?
How are you pushing us to seeking the change?

How fragile, how impermanence is real art!
Global crisis teaching how weak humans are
Will we prevent our own extinction as species
if fierce virus spread or if much bigger one comes!

How equal we are! In the eyes of Teacher Virus!
With no limits of race, religion or National borders
It doesn't care what colour we are, what language we speak
what history we hold, or what elatedness we at peak!

Nothing matters in the eyes of the contagious disease
In human suffering, pain of loss, all are just equal
We are at the loss of control, destiny or mastering our fate!
Corona busted the bubble of illusion with reality mastering!

In this suffering and death, humans became alone!
The pain that cannot be shared with loved ones in any way
Your health, your wellness, your pain or your death, it's just yours!
Isolation teaches you that end of the day it's just you to you what matters!

One mother could not see her dead son on other side of planet
A young man did not have the glimpse of his dead father!
There are no longer loved ones around mourning the loss
You are just a mass ready to be ash the minute the virus wins over you!

The Heart of a Poet

Time to understand the fear and the faith
Cherish whatever you before the moments of wraith
No wrong in reacting in our different way
Faith is not in the Stars or the Gods we pray

It is the human belief, that our wisdom can win
over the strength of the invisible virus vigorous dance
Realizing that we are so small and insignificant
Letting go greed, the human ego and all the fallacies of mankind

Time to join our hand in prayers in our countries and cities
Pray for medical teams and Government machinery in place
Keeping in thoughts of all those men and women already infected
Staying in homes and protecting our kith and kin

Today is still the day, we do not know what is tomorrow in store
Let's take THIS moment to shout out our love to those we mean
Call and ask up for that forgiveness to those who we did hurt
Take a moment to pause and show gratitude to all who meant for you

Corona crisis teaches us the loss of vanity of our lives
In midst of the existing madness, let's stay ground
not losing perspectives and things to fill our lives
For one day, this too shall pass, but the lessons not!

This global pandemic showed that no country is big
or no culture is supreme. All are just human species
Let's respect every living being with hope of tomorrow
so that we get back with hope and live again in true harmony!

Dr. Varsha Das writes fiction, non-fiction, poetry, radio plays and for children in Gujarati, Hindi and English and translates from Bangla, English, Gujarati, Hindi, Marathi and Odia. Her writing journey started in her teens. At 18, she received her first award from the Government of Gujarat. She was recognized through prizes from various institutions, including the Central Sahitya Akademi, Gujarati Sahitya Parishad and the Soka University. Her poems appeared in several anthologies in India and abroad. She is the former Director of National Book Trust (India), and served as the Director of the National Gandhi Museum after her retirement.

The Drawers

If I don't put something
at its designated place
I can never find it.
I lose my glasses everyday
And to look for them
Without wearing one
Is like searching for a black umbrella
in the dark room!

On one bright day
My daughter came up with an idea,
She got a tall cupboard made
With twenty odd drawers,
Wrote letters on each one
from A to Z.
And explained smilingly,
"Look Ma,
Now put your glasses in 'G',
And your pen in 'P'.
See, how simple it is!
There is no cause for worry!"
I also thought,
The idea was great
Glasses in 'G'
And pen in 'P',
My daughter is definitely
Brighter than me!

But just the other day,
a strange thing happened.
I picked up my glasses
from the drawer 'G'
And when I pulled 'P' for the pen
It was just not there!
Where can it disappear?
I did put it here!

The Conscious Poets

No, I am not going to panic.
I sat down quietly
pulled my daughter closer to me
holding her hand
I said calmly,
"Shut your eyes my child
And look within,
Is the life as simple
As the pen in 'P'?
And the glasses in 'G'?"

And there was a sudden flash of light,
I rushed to the drawer 'Q',
My dear pen cooed!
Wow! There it was,
it had no connection with 'Q'
but it stayed in, so calm and cool!

Said the 'Q' in gentle a voice,
"I agree, we are strangers,
we do make mistakes,
But I keep my heart warm,
and let her be in
till her dear one pulls the drawer
takes her lovingly."

My daughter, out of sheer curiosity
Rushed to the drawer 'H',
And found the heart there,
Beating and happy!
Then she pulled the drawer 'U'
saw the heart beating there too!
Whichever drawer she pulled
She saw the happy heart,
grinning and throbbing
in each one of them!

The Heart of a Poet

My child hugged me,
whispered in my ears,
"Yes Ma, you are right,
The one whose heart beats
In each drawer
Does not lose anything anywhere
EVER!"

Akash Sagar Chouhan has contributed to several anthologies with his poems and participated in poetry festivals, including Efflorescence by the Chennai Poetry Circle, Glomag by Glory Sasikala, The Virtual Reality (Sparrow Publishers), and the Guntur International Poetry Fest. He is a proud member of Soul Scriber's Society in Salem that organizes the Yercaud Poetry Festival every year.

A Stethoscope Reading of My Poem

One language,
Yet 195 pieces of hemmed land;
Resonating palpitations synchronize a mélange of colours to understand;
Undivided thoughts harbour at banks of unbiased minds,
Leave not the already left His in Her right hand.

Can they bribe a ceased heart to throb one more time,
Rehabilitate greed until torn pockets have infinite nothingness to pine and examine;
And in this ladder off and adds and for a sum total of ands,
Unsaid words truthfully lie to get unclenched as fist of sand.

Tomorrow is a ray of hope that does not need any cracked walls,
Light passes through abysmal wounds for each cavity calls;
Pen be a walking stick even before old age installs,
Who counts the empty scabbards?
After all how money edged swords and how many naked spades would fall?

An optimist, Dr. Hayim Abramson taught languages and Jewish studies. He has authored a book in Hebrew, *Shirat HaNeshamah*. His poems appeared in *Amaravati*: *Poetic Prism, Prosopisia, The Deronda Review, The Seventh Quarry, Voices*, and in e-zines. He participated in the *Contemporary World Haiku* and was a judge for the Poetry Contest of the Miriam Felicia Lindberg Memorial Foundation. Works of interest include sources of artistic inspiration; thoughts for HAIKU; notes on the Holocaust; Torah, the land and the Jewish people; the individual within the community; faith and outlooks on life.

http://www.hayimabramson.com

Exercising at the Beach

Today,

as in the good old days,

we trot and frolic by the sea.

We wave to the waves of time

that come and go

splashing that today

is the promised tomorrow

that we dreamed brighter shall be.

Tom Higgins was born in Egremont, Cumbria, UK and lives there sixty-six years later. He had a pretty "normal" upbringing, although not very materialistic, as his parents never seemed to have much money to spare. He is married and has two beautiful daughters, and now also has two lovely little grandsons. He wrote his first poem at the age of fifty-seven. He writes extensively now, but only when he feels he has something valid to say.

It Was Me, Guv'

It was you, and it was me
That's how this world came to be,
It was him and it was her
Who let everything occur,
It was us and it was them
Who got it wrong time and again.
None of us come out clean
Not the "kind" and not the "mean",
Not the stupid, not the wise,
The same rule to us all applies,
We all happily fell in ordered line
To queue for whatever is "mine, mine, mine".
We have all been watching, wide awake
We have all supported the real or the fake,
We have all followed the wrong or right,
And found ourselves now in blackest night
With no real vision to see us through the dark,
Perhaps now though, we'll see that spark,
That precious spark to make a bright new flame,
Which can transform this world of shame.

Born in Guelma, east of Algeria, Warda Zerguine is a poet, writer, researcher in the popular oral tradition, and a journalist. She has published four books on proverbs and popular puzzles and participated in numerous festivals in various cities in Algeria, Tunisia, Jordan, Lebanon and Morocco. She has contributed to different international anthologies in Tunisia, Indonesia, Serbia, India and Algeria with her work. She has written and recited many poems in different languages, including Arabic, English and French.

The Amorous Moon

I want to live in poetry
On a journey of paths of destiny
Affliction taught me
Revealing in my eyes
Treacherous spring
I have trebuchet dreamer
Restrained tears
I was looking for my rose
Under the moonlight
A beautiful time
A prosperous joy.

The Conscious Poets

From Portugal, Maria do Sameiro Barroso is a medical doctor and a multilingual poet, translator, researcher and an essayist in Portuguese and German Literature, translation studies and history of medicine. She has authored over 40 books of poetry, numerous translations and essays which were published in Portugal, Brazil, Spain, France, Serbia, Belgium, Albany, and USA. Her poems have been translated into over twenty languages. In 2020, she was awarded the Prize of the Académie Européene des Sciences, des Arts et des Lettres (AESAL).

The Dawn

I come up with the highest lights,
arising in the second last step
of the shadows;
my body wrapped in orange trees
loaded with leaves and birds.
The darkness is gone,
and also the wind and the rain.
In the glitter of ethereal images,
stealthy angels start coming out
among music, daffodils
and rain trumpets,
while I write down mazes
and long spirals.
In the magical and luminous hours,
I pour down my ink, my truth,
my myths and spells on broken
windows, empty shadows,
in sparkles of a primordial day.

The Conscious Poets

Aziz Mountassir has 6 poem collections in Arabic to his credit: *The Sad Melody*, *Play Waiting*, *Double Play*, *Pain*, *Scratches on the Waiting Face,* and *As Much as Fancy Comes*. His new poetry book, *Reproaching* is in print. His poems have been translated into various languages, including Amazigh, French, Spanish, Italian, Chinese, German, English, Filipino, Kurdish, Japanese, and Serbian as well as several other Slavic tongues. Some of his poems have been translated into Italian and composed as a musical piece.

An African Girl

I'm a lovely butterfly
My destiny is a thorny rose
I have nothing to do
except patience
and God is merciful
I suffer
I cry
Then I sleep
My pain is not only mine
Even the closest ones to me
Complain of my suffering
and they stay
in my cell
It's my pain and my misery
The misery of my father
Of my mother
Of my neighbours also
Oh, people of the world
Save me
I want my community
my brother
my friend
and my family
I'm dreaming of
My house
My garden
and my toys
Where's my school bag
My voice calls out
for the hymn of my country
Erase my tears
Bring a drink for my cough

Elizabeth Kurian 'Mona' writes and translates poetry in English, Hindi, Urdu, Telugu, and Malayalam. She has thirteen books, including translations, to her credit, some of which have been illustrated by Sushil Thapa, a well-known artist from Kathmandu, Nepal. Her poetry anthology *Beyond Images* has been translated into French by Supratik Sen and into Tamil by N. V. Subbaraman. Mona is the recipient of a number of literary awards. She has taken early retirement as Manager from the Reserve Bank of India, Mumbai. She is associated with various literary groups and is Secretary of the multilingual Sahitya Sangam International, Hyderabad.

monaliza.hyd@gmail.com

Hope Makes Life Livable

Every dark cloud does have a silver lining
Behind the clouds the sun keeps shining

Sorrow may come on his high horse riding
It knows not where happiness is hiding

Without hope, mankind would surely perish
With hope, great challenges do relish

None would have scaled lofty Mount Everest
If they had lost hope and went home to rest

Columbus wouldn't have crossed rough seas
If half way his will and courage would cease

In the gloom of despair would Pandora grope
If her gift box did not have the fairy of hope

The world faced floods, wars, a deadly virus
But like the Phoenix, from ashes of ruin rises.

Hussein Habasch, a poet from Afrin, Kurdistan, lives in Bonn, Germany. Some of his poems have been translated into many languages, including English, German, Spanish, French, Chinese, Turkish, Persian, Albanian, Uzbek, Russian, and Romanian. He has authored a large number of poetry books, and a selection of his poems have been published in numerous international anthologies. He participated in many international poetry festivals, including those that took place in Colombia, Nicaragua, France, Puerto Rico, Mexico, Germany, Romania, Lithuania, Morocco, Ecuador, El Salvador, Kosovo, Macedonia, Costa Rica, Slovenia, China, Taiwan, and New York City.

A Rose to the Heart of Life

Our madness to draw
Our madness to write
Our madness to give every day,
A rose to the heart of life
Our madness won't win my love!

Their madness to fight
Their madness to kill
Their madness to aim every day
A bullet to the heart of life
Their madness will win my love!

We will be defeated my love
I know that.
They will conquer my love
You know that.

But regardless we will draw,
write and give every day
A rose to the heart of life.

Translated by Muna Zinati

The Conscious Poets

Nguyen Chau Ngoc Doan Chinh, with her pen name Hong Ngoc Chau, is a native of Ho Chi Minh City, Vietnam. She has a master's degree in Education Management. She is a member of W. U. P (World Union of Poets) and is involved in numerous cultural and artistic activities. She has published two poetry books, *Vietnamese Contemporary Poetry* (Volume 1) and *The Couple of Terns in the Vast Sky*. She has various other printed works in newspapers, magazines and general publications to her credit.

NIỀM TIN KHÁT VỌNG

Cuộc đời luôn có lúc quay vòng
Hỡi khách trầm luân phút chạnh lòng
Hội ngộ phân ly ai biết trước?
Buồn vui ngày tháng biết mà trông?

Tâm tư chia sẻ chốn không tên
Ràng buộc chữ tình nên nợ duyên
Đôi trái tim yêu cùng nhịp đập
Nắng mưa từng trải những truân chuyên

Từ đây duyên nợ mong viên mãn
Sự nghiệp nhân sinh trọn ước nguyền
Tồn tại mai sau bao thế hệ
Niềm tin khát vọng vẫn triền miên

Yêu anh sống giản dị chân thành
Lý tưởng trào dâng giữa thế gian
Giữ lửa yêu thương cùng chí hướng
Lời thề chứng kiến có trời xanh.

The Belief of Aspiration

Life sometimes revolves in this existence
Let ask misery people in pondering moments
Who can foresee the reunion or separation?
Sad or joyful days so as to longing in motion?

We share confide at the nameless place
To tie our relationship being love fate
The two hearts in the same beat, same flow
Sunshine or rain we've ever experienced sorrows

From now on we hope our love fullness
Man life career adapts our desire more or less
For tomorrow, it exists throughout generations
It's forever constant the belief of aspiration

We love the simple life of sincerity
The ideal rises among life worldly
With our will, we keep our loving fire
The vow is witnessed by the blue sky

The Heart of a Poet

Additional Divisional Railway Manager (Pune), Neelam Saxena Chandra has 4 novels, 1 novella, 6 short story collections, 31 poetry collections and 13 children's books to her credit. She writes in English as well as Hindi. More than 1500 of her poems / stories have been published in various journals, anthologies and magazines. She holds a place in the 2015 Limca Book of Records for being the author having the highest number of publications in a year in English and Hindi. She has won several international and national awards. In 2014, Forbes listed her as one of the popular authors.

The Spring within You

You
Have a spring of energy
Flowing in the ravines of your soul.

The spring,
In its nascent stage of life,
Unaware of the potential energy it carries,
Hesitates in its path.
It doesn't know
That it shall one day
Transform into a beautiful and strong river.
Which shall give life
To many seeds on its banks,
Which shall be drunk
By humans and animals alike
Who will revere it with love;
Which shall even have the latent energy
To destroy forests and villages.

You
Should instill self-confidence
In the ability of the spring;
After all, in its growth,
Lies your power
To conquer the world
And also shift the horizons!

Ashok Bhargava has published five books of poetry. His poems have appeared in numerous anthologies worldwide. He is the recipient of the World Poetry Lifetime Achievement award. He finds living between cultures and languages highly intriguing and stimulating. He is the founder of WIN, the Writers International Network of British Columbia, Canada.

We Are When We Are

Why lose precious time
if there is nothing
meaningful to pursue

Follow the freshness of today
not the fragrance
of wilted flowers

Don't hang loose like
threads drying
crying hard

Create a new destiny
dream a new dream
yesterday won't return

Stoke the inner embers
to light
you wish to light

Life has no set meaning
simply live
and that will give it a meaning

The Heart of a Poet

Avril Meallem, a retired pediatric physiotherapist and complimentary therapist originally from London, UK, now lives with her husband in Jerusalem, Israel. Avril's poems have appeared in several Israeli and international online and printed anthologies, and she has received several Honorary Mentions in various competitions. She has authored *Dancing with the Wind* and *Come Sit with Me by the River*. She has co-authored two collections of *Tapestry Poetry*. This work is an innovative form of collaborative poetry writing that Meallem developed together with Shernaz Wadia of India.

http://www.avrilm.webs.com
http://www.tapestrypoetry.webs.com

The Antenna of Trust

Almond and almond blossoms nod their sleepy heads,
covering the waiting earth below
in carpets of pink and white…
nature, so gentle, yet so full of pain
from the human battles raged within her arms,
so much blood absorbed into her fertile soil,
so many words of hate, jealousy,
unforgiveness, wafted on the wind.

But we have been so blind in our search for progress,
have encircled our world with a web of angry energy.
If only we could now, as an offshoot of the pandemic,
open our eyes to see beyond the physicality of our existence.

I see a swirling mist of crimson light filling all space,
a light of love, flowing from the beating heart of the Creator.
We only have to reach out beyond our minds,
connect to this light as a radio, when turned on,
can be tuned into a specific channel.

Let us each fine-tune our own antennae of trust,
draw down God's gift into our whole being,
allowing the crimson light of love to radiate
a joy never before known by mankind,
a joy of the original *Gan Eden**.

*Garden of Paradise

The Heart of a Poet

Kamar Sultana Sheik mostly writes on spirituality, mysticism and nature with a focus on Sufi poetry. A post-graduate in the field of Botany, she received her education from the St. Aloysious Anglo-Indian School and completed her degree at SIET Women's College (Chennai). Throughout her career of 18 years, she worked with various organizations and institutions, including the IT sector. She is a self-styled life coach, and currently concentrates on her writing fulltime. She has contributed to various anthologies with her poems and won several prizes in poetry contests. A green enthusiast, blogger and content-writer, Sultana calls herself "a wordsmith".

sultana_sheik@yahoo.co.in

The Heart of a Poet

The poet is a wordsmith
His toolbox is a full-house;
Hammering a word here,
Hitting the nail on the head!

The poet is a painter,
Drawing word pictures
He colours his works of art,
With the finest brushes of metaphor;
The poet is a gardener,
Growing flowers of simile and idiom
In unfading bloom,
For posterity.

The poet is a potter,
Molding the clay of language,
Embellishing it with choicest vocabulary
Molding pots and pans of experience
At the wheel of poesy.

The poet is a glassworker,
Giving fairy shapes
To visions and dreams
Awakening in the glass of inspiration
The element of ether.

The poet is a weaver,
Stitching sound, melody and sonnet
Into the fabric of verse and rhyme
Making timeless tapestries.

The poet is a Seeker,
Of a strange wanderlust;
In losing his way he finds
The path to all hearts

The Heart of a Poet

And his own.
Riding on the flimsiest moonbeam,
Reaches realms unthread on foot;
Then stands, showing the way
For those who care to follow;
Methinks, when all the birds have sung and gone
And angels fell silent,
The Creator wanted
A different music,
He created a Poet.

Sujan Bhattacharyya is a poet, novelist and an essayist from India. While he mostly writes in Bengali – his mother language, he often takes up English to express his inner feelings. His work appears frequently in well-known Bengali literary periodicals. He has several published literary titles to his credit. As a writer and poet, he is marked with his crude realism and a strong optimistic view.

Towards a New Course

Whom shall we say?
From whom shall we flee away
To the nascent dawn
When the mankind knew to cast his head high?

We are the speakers,
And surely the noble audience that
Only we make.
Where're the words. The softest expression
Of our desired path?
Keep the distance safe, panics the Globe.
Don't approach me so near
So that I'm trembled.

How far can we go apart?
How deep can we tear our masks?
A tiny virus is reigning the earth,
Putting us all in a slumber social.

Once we slept, shall wake up together all.
Once we're hurt, shall recover from that wound.
Rightly we're keeping a distance physical;
But our hearts are beating together
In the valleys, shores, forests and man-made towns.

There's no humanity without living hearts.
There's no society without bondage of love.
Keep me bodily apart,
But don't forget to keep me in your heart.

If it be a pandemic now,
The coming morn will be a human one.

Aditi Roy is an ardent reader who loves reading romantic tragedies, essays, short stories and poems. In addition to reading, she is interested in photography and painting. She studied journalism, and has an M.A. in English Literature from Calcutta University. She is a content writer by profession, and writing is food for her soul. She has contributed to many popular online magazines with her stories and poetry, but also to international anthologies.

Let's Give Hope a Chance to Bloom

She's beautiful
She's warm
She's lovely
She's a protector against odds
But, she our mother earth, now sick has borne enough storms, over the years.

She doesn't show her tears
That doesn't mean she can't cry
She wants to scream out her heart in pain
But, in silence she helplessly pines inside.

She has questions filled in her eyes
But, she wants to know where hope resides?

Hope, comes from the ashes of huge loss and grows like a lone sapling
Hope, carves its way out of a heart full of tragedy and bears a heavy cost.

Hope, rises like a soldier rising from war zone, trying to return to his mother at home.

Hope, is like a clear and calm sky after a stormy night

Even Pandora opened its box full of calamities
That inflicted humanity
Questioning hope's originality

Only giving hope a chance to bloom
Will help overcome all misery very soon.

Gino Leineweber was born in 1944 in Hamburg, Germany. He has been active as a writer since 1998. In addition to short stories, travel books and biographies, he has published poetry books in English and German, and was honored with several international awards for his poetry. He has edited three international poetry anthologies. Since 2013, he has been serving as President of the Three Seas Writers' and Translators' Council, which is based in Rhodes, Greece. He is a member of the PEN-Centre German-Speaking Writers Abroad (former German Exile-PEN).

The Odor of Life

No borders no limits no age

The madness which is in
The odor of life
Has ceased my silliness
I now inhale
Smells from the fall
The forest is already in sight
The sun that has shone so long
Appears only veiled
Behind the fragrance of trees

I am walking further
Though the winter is coming
I am going through

There is another spring

Zaldy Carreon De Leon, Jr. is an internationally noted creative writer with degrees in both secular and ecclesiastical schools. His literary work appears in various local and international journals. He is a licensed teacher, researcher, translator and theologian. He is an active member of the Global Academy for Human Excellence, an international humanitarian group.

I, a Little Tree . . .

Am I.
The vast waters reach far
But the wind catches its debris dews for me,
The sun from a distant place is fiery,
My leaves won't live long from its tongues of fire,
But the clouds filter that I may live
Another day, another night, indeed.

The vast waters and the sun,
The wind and the clouds,
These are the things that made me grow.
My roots may one day reach a deeper mile,
And my leaves outgrow to heavenward,
But I know, I cannot,
For in this world, I need not indifference!

My roots are short, it won't lead a depth,
My leaves will wither after some days,
But I, a little tree am I, a tree spiritual,
The wind, the clouds, the ghost, is one.
The world is vast for my wearing time,
Who should replace me from where I stand?

A young man to an old man, said,
Wearing down soils and dust,
everyone complied,
The need for tomorrow is always implied,
But of tears and joy,
is everybody's wine,
Where the moon hides,
time is there confined.

In the darkest hour,
our soul may have done
Nothing but our hands can work in a time,
Of manifold eyes,
who saw how it is to be man
When there is a need to,
our hearts rhyme.

The Conscious Poets

Of certainty, the face of yesterday is old,
Her happiness and losses, is thus behold,
If we forget the spirit,
if we decline from its dust,
We are nothing but human,
a living bust.

The old man to the young man replied,
What surrounds us may never be right
Burden and tears, weeping eyes,
Where is that manifold light
Filtering the day for someone's rise.

For he who tends his brother's arm
To turn the ease back to him again
Is heaven's calm beneath a storm,
To be free again, a broken chain.

I therefore say, with utmost joy,
Keep this day tact as I demand,
For today you have to employ
A good work that bears a fruitful end.

Today, a pure white vase is my keeper,
Tomorrow let it be broken...
Let it be broken, so I may resume
A fate intended for me,
O not for glory, O not for power,
But to scatter my fruits around,
O for a depth, and O for height,
My dreams survive, when the vase begone.

All in perfect time, when the hour comes,
The world will be fruitful.
Full of hope, I pray, I cried,
I am just a small piece of God's creation,
But let me do my work though
I, a tree . . .
am I.

The Heart of a Poet

Aneek Chatterjee is a poet and an academic from Kolkata, India. He has a Ph.D. in International Relations and has been teaching in leading Indian and foreign universities. His poems have appeared in reputed literary magazines and poetry anthologies across the globe, including the *Chiron Review*, *Shot Glass Journal*, *The Stray Branch*, *Chicago Record*, *Ann Arbor Review*, *Dissident Voice*, *Café Dissensus*, *Setu*, *Ethos Literary Journal*, *New Asian Writing*, *Pangolin Review*, *Montreal Writes*, and *Mark Literary Review*. He has two books of poems to his credit, *Seaside Myopia* and *Unborn Poems and Yellow Prison*.

Hope

When mud covered
bones & flesh in days of yore,
sudden rains splashed joy, hope

The lonely beck meandering through
marshy lands without ease
always cheered me

When the drowsy road felt guilty
for pestilence, yellow bushes dripped
paintings & whispered love

The milky way told in an orange evening
hope is not just a four-letter word,
it's found everywhere in the galaxy

An Architecture Planner, Shruti Goswami has numerous English poems in several national and international anthologies and on poetry websites. Her Bengali stories have been published in magazines and some appear in *Bengali Daily*. *Navotthan* showcases some of her translations, and she writes regularly for banglalive.com. Her poems have been recited in online poetry shows in Canada. She has two poetry books to her credit, *Another Soliloquy* (2014) and *Solitary Corner* (2019). She has acted in short films, composed poems for two Bengali short films, and translated Bengali short film scripts into English. Her favourite pastime is reading and travelling.

Phoenix

Lonely roads
Desert sands envelope
Caressing their hunger;

Flowers breathe a soul
Before withering away
Like a prayer sent home.

An eerie silence prevails
Laughter robbed away
Bustling streets, pavement,
Walkways weep;
And the breeze
No longer whispers
Across meadows and trees:
Fear reigns
Warriors in masks tiptoe
Where angels fear to tread
Time creeps like a snail;

Suddenly, drops of rain
Kissing like a lost child found again
And hope reigns
The sun still shines, everyday
The rains and breeze
Still make the trees sway
To the music of life.
Life is a Phoenix;
Life goes on.

Chijioke Ogbuike is a Chartered Accountant, and this is how he puts food on the table. He has varied aspirations in the arts. As a poet, he has a self-published anthology of fifty poems, *Pregnant Thoughts*. He also has a self-published novel, *Expelled* which can be found online. He is a musician who plays under the pseudonym 'Don Ketchy' and has two albums, *fortune n the slave* and *A cut above the rest* – with the third in the wings. Both recordings are available online. He is married with children. He lives in Lagos, Nigeria.

Each One Teach One

Wisdom will never be a common commodity like left over oat meals on a morning we woke up hungry and late
Foolishness will also not be reserved for a particular many in society nor for a season that passes without debate
There is an equal measure of both between wakefulness and sleep
As startling in contrast as want is to need
Life is as life is
And humanities best aspiration will always be to fan the embers that fuel their wish
In the drudgery of this existence
Flights of fancy is also a common pence
We forget we are made of dreams
Because we are half consumed with listening to the allures that is not what it seems
Our forgotten history which is most important is our shared humanities,
and that we come from a mother
Where goes all your aspirations if it does not identify with its societies,
are you just a number?
Larger than life but not so large as to spill over a square piece of earth
bedding six feet deep
For this is what it's all about when one day we will fail to wake up from sleep
Every child eventually becomes old
As everything secret will eventually be told
The only wealth therefore is the one we share
Because when the passing comes it does not spare
All of us that read this are but a continuing reason
Why we can only become better by helping each other see that season
Teach me then rather than vilify me
To be comfortable in another's discomfort is a denial of this connectedness of we
For this ecosphere, we know to transform
Each one here must teach one
Teach me then rather than leave me
This humanity is restored for every moment we chose to side with the you that is in me.

The Heart of a Poet

Lucky Stephen Onyah, a poet, an entrepreneur and a public speaker, is a Lagosian by birth. He is a Mathematics teacher and Principal at the Genii Field College and an English teacher at the World English Institute.

The Dawn of Hope

Darkness prevails at night
Joy comes with dawn in sight
None can attain by fight
For fear make all take flight
Do pray to God for might

Sunrise brings hope again
Ruins all that drives insane
Acing all cause of pain
Labour with hope for gain
God's promise does retain

Go! Sow your seeds with joy
All good things come with toil
With hope, care for the soil
Your reward none can spoil
A great law none can foil

Do reap as you labour
These moments do savour
Repay toils with favours
Be kind to your neigbours
God make you a saviour

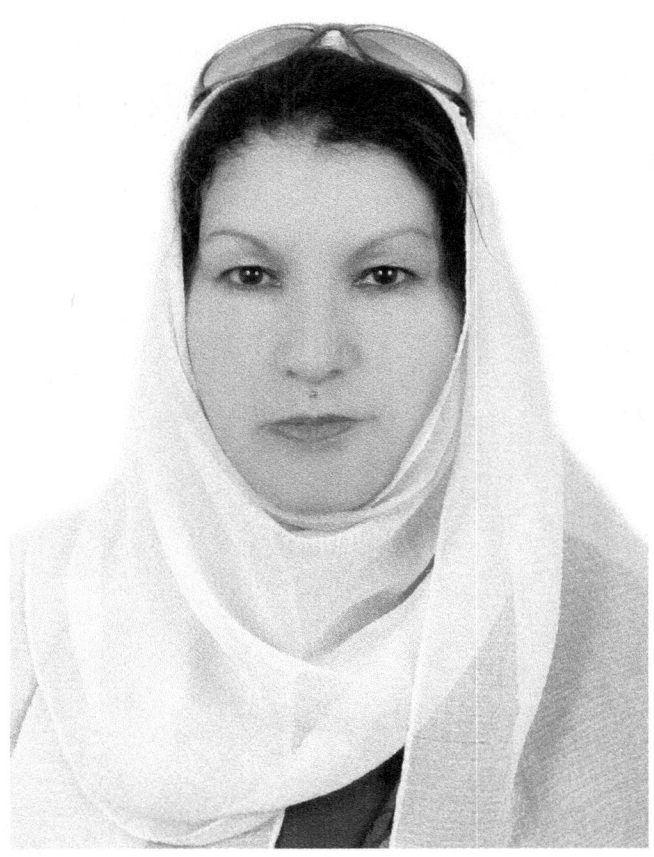

A native of Casablanca who lives in Safi, Morocco, Izza Fartmis studied English Literature at Mohamed V University in Rabat. She is a retired teacher of English and won, as a former International Connecting Classrooms Coordinator, the 2012 International School Award for her school. She is a member of the League of Women Writers of Morocco and has contributed to various international anthologies with her poems, including *Amaravati Poetic Prism* (three times) and Inner Child Press International's *Corona . . . Social Distancing*. Izza writes in Arabic, French and English, and has five books (poetry and prose) to her credit.

Izza.fartmis@gmail.com

Climb the Wall

Climb the wall,
It's not hard at all
To try your pith
And look over it,
You won't see an abyss
Nor any reeking bones;
But a flourishing oasis,
A balmy greenhouse,
You'll pick up flowers,
Within your reach,
Those gone to seed
And get down with a will
To break the dam
Then extend its heavenly
Spice to your land
Strewed with fertile grains,
You'll grow worth
In different colors,
The bright and dark ones,
As part of life, together
They'll take to one another.

The Heart of a Poet

Mamu Roshid, a budding Rohingya Poet from Myanmar, loves to write poems, short stories and quotes. He emerged as a prominent love-poet on social media. Mamu has participated in several poetry competitions, receiving prizes. Several organizations have recognized him as a poet and a humble servant of humanity. His poems appeared in numerous international anthologies.

Being Human

As a human being you want to get freedom.
To be able to create and discover yourself
A person regardless of the judgment of others.
Being human also helps you do good.

Being human accepting everything that you are and living
Your life in a way without regret or worry.
Being human and showing passion.
Crying when you are upset or crazy, laughing like a maniac.

Making human mistakes and being faulty.
Being human something
Pounds, unhealthy occasional eating, and stress breakouts.
Human split ends and other things

Being human making friends,
Then they have your back
Discovery of all being human
He is around you and is traveling to the globe.

As a human being, it helps you in everything you do,
But also realize that when enough is enough.
Being human, the differences are set aside
Together with those people you never thought you could.

The Heart of a Poet

Kamala Wijeratne is a well-known educator, writer and poet from Sri Lanka. She works with the National Institute of Education and the Ministry of Education on national curriculum development. She authored her first poetry book in 1983. Her twelve poetry and three short fiction books have been published in and outside Sri Lanka. For two of the latter, she received State Literary Awards in addition to her poetry prizes in 2004 and 2018. In 2019, she was distinguished with a lifetime achievements award, "Sahithyarathna", for her contributions to English language literature. Her poems appear in the curriculum of various universities.

https://www.facebook.com/wijeratne.kamala

https://sites.google.com/site/kamalawijeratne/

Not the End but an Intermission

Let's not think
This is the end
But an intermission
To rethink old gradations
Review old classifications

It's time to stop thinking of severed worlds
The developed with everything gainable
The developing aspiring to gain
And the Undeveloped with no gains

Let's talk instead
Of those who ravaged and raped
Those who spoiled the earth
Those who poisoned the water
Those who polluted the air
Denuded the forests
Killed its denizens
And enjoyed its goodness
By themselves

And those others
Who were gentle
To their Mother
Who respected her laws
Who obeyed her strictures
Loved her loveliness
And lived side by side
With other earthlings
And we're content
With their lives

Let's rethink old gradations
Review old classifications
And move on.

Kapardeli Eftichia lives in Patras, Greece. She studied journalism and has a Ph.D. from the Arts and Culture World Academy. She holds a chair in Greek Culture at the University of Cyprus. She writes poetry, short stories, HAIKU and essays. She has received many awards from national competitions, and has contributed to numerous national and international anthologies with her poems. She is a member of the World Poets Society, IWA (International Writers and Artists Association) and Poetas del Mundo, which recognized her with a certification in 2017 as the "Best Translator".

http://world-poets.blogspot.com
https://www.facebook.com/kapardeli.eftichia

ΕΛΠΙΣ

Οι δεσμώτες ξόδεψαν
όλον τον Ήλιο
και η Άνοιξη δεν ξύπνησὲ ποτέ
***
Η ελπίδα γεμάτη στολίδια
κατοικεί σε όλους τους
τόπους
στην αιωνιότητα της μοναξιάς
μιας απόφασης ημέρα
ξυπνώ
***
Τα χρώματα
μοιάζουν αληθινά
στον τοίχο του ονείρου
με της φωτιάς τα κατακόκκινα ρόδα
στις φτερούγες των πουλιών
στη μέση του κόσμου
μαζί της θα φύγω

Hope

The guards spent
around the Sun
and Spring who never woke

Hope
full of ornaments
resides in all
sites
I wake
a day decision
eternity of loneliness

The Colours
look really in
in the wall of dream
with fire bright red roses
the wings of birds
in the middle of the world
with her
I will leave

Olfa Philo Drid, who holds a Ph.D. in American Literature, is a poet, playwright and translator from Tunisia. Her work has appeared in many international anthologies and literary journals. Some of her poems were translated into more than 12 languages and some were composed as Italian songs, performed by Fabio Martoglio. In 2018, the Motivational Strips Academy distinguished her as one of the World's Top Six Writers with "The Connoisseur De Poetry Award". Olfa has a play and two poetry collections to her credit.

https://www.youtube.com/channel/UChMcYZtsitYOCixxYM5Kz5g

A Republic Somewhere

I once dreamt of a republic
where poets are the legislators,
politicians are the cleaners and where
candidates for presidency are elected
according to their fame as writers . . .

I once dreamt of a republic
where rulers are writers and poets
and where taxes are collected to
help creative disadvantageous writers
publish their books and reach larger audience . . .

I once dreamt of a republic
where banknotes are used as handkerchiefs,
and where people are required to pay their purchases
with poems and if ever they feel short of inspiration,
they can pay with a bundle of flowers instead . . .

I once dreamt of a republic
where doctors cure their fellow human beings free of charge
except for the prayers their receive from those ailing patients
and the gifts they could afford to offer them . . .

I once dreamt of a republic
where social classes are divided according to the color of hearts;
where the upper-class people are the ones with the whitest hearts
while the lower- class people are the ones with the blackest hearts . . .

I once dreamt of a republic
where football players are marginalized and in case of need,
they are invited to entertain people for free before big cultural events
and receive nothing in exchange except awards, medals and cups . . .

I once dreamt of a republic
where lawyers are obliged to defend
the oppressed for free and expect nothing
in exchange except God's blessings . . .

The Conscious Poets

I once dreamt of a republic
where sex is prohibited and couples are allowed
to exchange only compliments, caresses, kisses and hugs
and are taught by a spiritual guru how to contain their sexual drives
and how to transcend their animalistic needs . . .

I once dreamt of a republic
where married couples are obliged to wear identical clothes
like twins each day to keep remembering the solemn oath they swore
on their wedding day to remain forever two souls in one . . .

I once dreamt of a republic
where criminals are punished by doing labors to soften their hearts
like taking care of senile people and orphans or helping charity
organizations in their mission of humanizing the world . . .

I once dreamt of a republic
where high-tech gadgets are broken into pieces
and people are obliged to devote themselves to the beings
surrounding them instead of the alien ones across the ocean . . .

I once dreamt of a republic
where bars are destroyed and replaced instead
by sports centers to which depressed people go
to relieve stress and anxiety in a healthy way . . .

I once dreamt of a republic
where gossipers and enviers are arrested and jailed
and they are punished each morning by being obliged
to drink detergent products to cleanse
their mouths, bodies, hearts and souls . . .

I once dreamt of a republic
where sorcerers and witches are burned in fire
together with their dangerous esoteric books and talismans
to say halt to those unprovable horrible crimes committed
with the help of their worshipped devils!

The Heart of a Poet

I once dreamt of a world
where people travel without passports

and everywhere they go, they find their fellow human(e) beings
to provide them with food and shelter . . .

I once dreamt of a world
where people are not allowed to expose their religions
and are called to practice their rituals secretly in their homes
and let their behaviors (not appearance) reflect their good or evil nature . . .

I once dreamt of a world
where the demonic vibes of power, wealth and control of the masses
suddenly metamorphosed into angelic vibes of empathy, sympathy
love and peace overwhelming each and every nation . . .

Orbindu Ganga, a post-graduate in sciences, is the first recipient of the Dr. Mitra Augustine gold medal for academic excellence. He worked in financial, banking, and publishing domains and has proven his finesse as a Soft Skills Trainer and Content Account Manager (Client Relationship Manager). Orbindu is a multilingual poet, author, critic, content writer, sketch artist, researcher, and spiritual healer. He has authored the book, *SAUDADE* and two research papers on poetry. His poems have appeared in many international publications and anthologies. His painting and articles have been published in *Awakening*, a spiritual journal.

Being Humane

Tectonic plates have opened
To swallow, the greedy souls,
Waves have plummeted from
The sea, to skim the firmament,
Unknown and unseen plagued
The throat, cleaving the being,
Wrath of nature have pummeled
Many times, to let us know her ire,
She made many endeavors
To change us, for a new dawn to rise,
We ignored her without looking
At her, to face the repercussion,
Remorse has veined in deep
Clutching him, to accept our mistakes,
With many souls leaving us
With our greed, we imbibed for ages,
Time has shown us the lesson
Not to imitate, the mistakes in the future,
The inception of tomorrow is beautiful
In our children, being loved and cared,
Removing the dust darted for so long
Within our self, for a better tomorrow,
Loving the misted droplets falling
On the leaf, to sprinkle from east,
Showers lifted the passion to flow
In her veins, kissed by the arteries,
Thoughts are shifting from loving
The notes, to see the smile in others,
Appreciating life is seen with misted eyes
To hold the dear ones, close to our heart,
Showing compassion is being the way
To see bliss within, changing the norm,
Humanity has risen from the mayhem
To see the human, with love and care.

Basab Mondal is a teacher from Kalkata, with unbridled affection for literature. He loves poetry, irrespective of language. He holds an M.A. in English Literature and Education, and writes to gratify his own inner self.

Metamorphosis

Tame the hungry crabs,
Burn the withering bones,
Mix your own colours,
Design the seasons, with
fresh bred chlorophyll.

Rise,
Rise, unlike Gregor Samsa,
Denying,
The Oracle of Fate.

The Conscious Poets

Born in 1983 in the eastern part of Bhutan, Phuntsho Wangchuk is an aspiring and budding poet. He graduated from a teacher-training college in Bhutan in 2009 and is currently pursuing his M. A. in English at Yonphula Centenary College. He loves reading and writing poems and songs that mirror the mundane lives and mindsets. He writes lyric poems of various forms on satirical themes. His poetry is mostly descriptive as well as dramatic, which rapturously appeals to the senses of the readers. An undaunted bosom-friend of nature, Wangchuk strives to promote social peace and harmony through his writings.

The Song of Hope

In the desert of despair, Hope vegetates still,
And with broken bits of life, he builds wings
To fly on the shadow of darkness, over a hill,
And writes a song of sunshine that he sings
Cheerfully like a robin sings wish for springs.

Sometimes, in clinic wards, Hope is figured
With patients, patting his solace at their rear;
He oft rises like a ghost, tired and meagered,
From the grave of shattered dreams to cheer
Those broken hearts, pained by dreaded fear.

Lo! There Hope rambles in the barren streets,
Searching his friends; in an empty classroom
Then he sits. Hark! In wishful voice, he greets
His teacher yet forlorn, ready to learn abloom
Despite being frazzled by learning from zoom.

Hope warbles his song in quarantined places,
Longing for home; he's in the lock-down seen,
Perching on the stained, desperate grimaces;
In the lands where people lost jobs umpteen,
There he sings to bring on their faces, a sheen.

In the sacred heart of kings and in the broken
Houses, Hope sings so loud, far beyond eyes,
For orphans and widows as his healing token;
So he sings, "hope never dies, hope never dies,
It may be torn or shattered, but again it'll rise!"

Divya Sinha is from Delhi, India. After 30 years of service in the central government, she retired in May, 2015. She had many stories and poems running through her head for years, which she began to put on paper recently. Her work includes poetry for the disadvantaged children she teaches.

A Little Missive

A little missive from me to you,
Yet to come and occupy the stage we do.
You and I and creatures all,
Go through life just seeking happiness
Old-fashioned, isn't it?
Out of date, ancient, prehistoric.
Judgmental were we, as you will be.

When the virus goes away
And we take a stock of what remains,
I hope we bequeath to you
This blue sky,
With wisps of clouds floating like cotton.
White little butterflies flocking to orange-red gulmohar blooms,
The majestic kites gliding in the sky.
The emerald of new leaves in spring,
The sunbird frolicking on the round, fluttering leaves,
Under the water dripping from a drainpipe,
Like a maiden under a waterfall.
The bulbul swaying in the wind on the tip of a banana branch,
Screeching parrots of green svelte bodies,
Their beaks painted in bright red lipstick.
And when I wake up in your brave new world.
Like a Rip Van Winkle,
Ignorant of your language,
Innocent of your technology,
You and I still have in common,
This blue sky, and dream under the stars
And look at the Venus there
As did I from my bedroom window,
As did our stone age ancestor.
Smile at the butterflies sashaying in your garden,
Smell the fragrant frangipani,
And when you read "The Lady of Shallot"
You share her pain as did I.

Dr. Anuradha Bhattacharyya is a writer from India. In 2016 and 2019, she received the Best Book Award for English Novels from the Chandigarh Sahitya Akademi. She is an Associate Professor of English in Sector 11 of the Postgraduate Government College in Chandigarh.

The Warrior

It matters not
Who pulled your leg
And dashed your dreams to the ground;
It matters not how heavily
You were wounded;
How cruelly your assets
Have been snatched away,
How desperately you needed them.
It matters not
What you were in the past,
What you had achieved,
How your ladder has been
Hacked away from below.
All the things you had
Were not destined to last;
They have pulled you up so far
And they have done their job . . .
From where your leg dangles
Over the deep chasm
Haul yourself with a masterful stroke
That the world has not seen yet
And would be amazed to watch now –
From that panting pull
Draw all others in who dwell
In the darkness below
And never mind
If one of them was also that
Who first pulled your leg.

Sunil Sharma, a senior academic, writer, critic, poet, freelance journalist, is from Mumbai, India. So far, he has published 22 books on prose, poetry and criticism – some of them having been co-authored. Sunil edits the monthly bilingual publication, *Setu*.

http://www.setumag.com/p/setu-home.html
http://www.drsunilsharma.blogspot.in/

The Perspective of a Bedouin

Spring erupts in a desert!

Few flowers bedeck the red-brown dunes, the evening moon
lends a sense of unreal to the heaving sands
of time watched by a
Bedouin in that harsh land.

A calm night waits in the sky
Tomorrow is in its womb.
Future is future, mere tense

rooted in present, another tense
a way of measuring time!

Storms come and go
but the desert, sea and moon
remain constant in the long
journey of humankind; an evolutionary species
that survives so many ages---ice and bronze and many others---in
its strides towards modernity.

Worst,
Best,
Worst-best
travelers have to be calm
and
in a shifting landscape,
hope shines, as the morning dew drops
glitter on the moveable surfaces
and

that is life
yours and mine, on this planet!

Dr. Tzemin Ition Tsai (蔡澤民博士), from Taiwan, is a professor at the Asia University and editor-in-chief of *Reading, Writing and Teaching Academic Texts*. He regularly writes columns for the *Chinese Language Monthly* in Taiwan. In his literary work, Tsai focuses on the description of nature, the anatomy of emotion and humanity, lifetime writing, graphic writing, and cross-domain writing. He is a scholar with a wide range of expertise and maintains a common and positive interest in sciences, engineering and literature. His writings appeared in anthologies, books, journals, and newspapers in more than 40 countries.

Chanting for Falling Flowers

There was a long time
I thought that poem
Just to show gorgeous
Or just to show good qualities
Better than
The bright moon at night

There was a long time
I thought that poem
Just to help others laugh
Or just to suppress the sadness of parting
Dispatching the loyalty of emotions
Made the evil spirits and the gods sad

Great conjecture, since
Only I understood in the world
Your thin and beautiful frame
Was as pretty as the poignant beauty of plum blossoms
Only you knew in the world
I have looked the messages in poetry lighter and lighter
No longer complaining that the good-looking was so easy to die away
Beyond this mortal world
Why, I
Needed to hold up this black nib
Created all this endless spring, boundless thinking

An independent Chartered Accountant, S. Sundar Rajan is a published poet and writer. His books, *Beyond the Realms* (poetry) and *Eternal Art* (short stories in English) have been translated into Tamil, Malayalam, Hindi and Telugu. Every weekend, The Kalpakkam Community Radio Station broadcasts his *Sundara Kadhaigal* (short stories in Tamil). His writings of varied themes carry a universal message. He edits *Madras Hues, Myriad Views* (a prose and poetry anthology). A catalyst for social activities and a nature lover, Rajan has recently initiated tree planting in his neighbourhood. He lives his life true to his motto, "Boundless Boundaries Beckon".

sundarrajan@srsmanagement.net

Musings of a Bird

My second home is nestled in a tree,
With a river calmly flowing carefree,
Brings scintillating music to the ear,
Along with the rustling leaves, in top gear.
This year I see a sea change in the air,
So refreshing, that one could for aspire.
The sky is bereft of smog on our flight,
The Earth presents a heavenly sight.
Never in our earlier days we've seen,
In our flight from our home, such joyous scene.
There is a strange quietness all around,
With humanity all gone underground.
Oh! An unpolluted atmosphere,
Hope this sustains across the sphere.
Nature has again quietly spelt it out,
Co-existence is the best way, no doubt.

*This poem was written to celebrate the World Migratory Bird Day on May 9, 2020.

Jyoti Kanetkar is a writer and poet who has received national and international awards for her work. Her four short story collections and two collections of poems have been published in India, the UK, Canada and the US. She writes in English and Marathi. Her poems, stories, essays and articles have appeared in numerous anthologies, including those by the *Destine Literare Magazine* (Canada) and *Inner Child Press International* (the US). She continues to contribute to literature, art and culture journals with her literary writings.

The Victor

I rise again. No one knows
Who I am. The strong one
The Victor. The secret self.
Confident, beauteous, sensual
Spiritual, purposeful.

Above all clear in the mind
About the direction to follow.
The steps to take to make
Every coveted dream come
True.

Maybe a few know a little
Of the truth – those who
Had the good fortune to
Walk a few steps of my
Journey with me.

I arise this morning refreshed,
Empowered, splendidly alone,
Towering above life itself;
Dwarfing the Phoenix in the
Splendour of regeneration.

I am in tune to the beat
Of my victory. Marching
Into the blazing light –
Forever the Winner.

Kamani Jayasekera is an only child of academics who exposed her to the world of the word from early childhood on. She is a graduate of The University of Kelaniya, minoring in English and specializing in Western Classical Culture, and has a master's and doctoral degree from the same university. Presently, she teaches Classics in both Sinhala and English in her alma mater as a senior professor. She has written many books for her field in both languages. Her passion, however, seems to be for creative writing. She received several awards for her short stories and poems in English.

Examples of Rebuilding
Taking an example from the bees ~ Virgil

It was not only the enemies-the wasps
That disturbed their existence, but nature
Itself in the form of wild winds and
gusts of dust, and humans with their torches
Agitation using smoke with the intention
of cruel exploitation, knowing very well
How we had exerted ourselves in building.

What planning and organizing of energy
That had united to build, to gather and
Produce the collection of nourishment
Sparkling , healthy and tasty- the very reason
For the attacks most unkind. Where the
Inhabitants were forced to protest with
Loud buzzing arising from their innermost self.

Yet dispersing in dismay at a fistful of sand
Thrown among them, Though refusing to accept
Defeat, for their revenge would be, they knew
Was to rebelliously rebuild and display
Their strength of solidarity and recreate
A bee comb oozing with the sweetest of honey
Setting an example to all humanity.

Kimberly Burnham has a Ph.D. in Integrative Medicine. She lived in Colombia; in Belgium during the Vietnam War; in Japan, teaching English to businessmen; in Toronto, and several places in the US. She resides in Spokane, WA with her wife, Elizabeth, two sets of twins (age 11 & 14) and three dogs. Her book, *See Faster, Vision Exercises for Basketball Players* helps athletes with eyesight issues. Kim's poetry weaves through *Awakenings: Peace Dictionary*; *Language and the Mind, a Daily Brain Health Program*; *Inspired by Gandhi, A Woman's Place in the Dictionary* and 79 volumes of *The Year of the Poet*.

https://www.nervewhisperer.solutions/

A Vision of Home in the Whole World

Happy when we all feel safe at home
with the people we cherish
we share our life

Happy when we all feel safe at home
in our garden and the natural world around us
we share our creativity with birds and bees

Happy when we all feel safe at home
in the warmth of diverse communities
we share in the brilliance of every religion, race, and culture

Happy when we all feel safe at home
as the world shares in the rest
from the frenzied pace of human commerce

Happy when we all see our place at home
with family, living creatures and community
we share in all the abundance and joy of this world

Happy when we all see that there is enough
chocolate, love, land, food
when we share

Ibrahim Honjo is a poet, writer, sculptor, painter, photographer and property manager. His poems have appeared in numerous journals and newspapers and broadcast in radio stations in Yugoslavia, Canada and the USA. He writes in English and Serbo-Croatian. Honjo received several prizes for his poetry. He has 30 books to his credit (21 in Serbo-Croatian and 9 in English) and contributed to more than 30 anthologies with his poems. Some of his work has been translated into Korean, Slovenian, Polish, Spanish, Italian, Mongolian, German and Bahasa (a Malaysian language).

Trinity

I was born on a stone
under that star
below which it does not grow
poisonous plants

poison has always been brought
from the west and the east
it sits below the star
under which it easily succeeded
and hated greed

by ethnicity, I am a Man
my nationality is Earthen
and faith Love

I live and I do not leave a trace
which other people will follow
everybody has traces that blindly follow

It is my right and my duty
to not stop from my way
and to get back under the rock
under that star
below which no poison is growing up

only words will remain behind me
Man, Earthen, Love
as a sacred trinity
conceived
withered and died with me
and in me

The Conscious Poets

Alicia Minjarez Ramírez is an internationally renowned Mexican poet and translator who has won numerous awards, including The World Cultural Excellence Award (2020) of the government of Peru, The Excellence Prize World Poetry Championship (Romania, 2019), Literary Prize "Tra le Parole e L'infinito" (Italy, 2019), and the EASAL Medal from The European Academy of Sciences and Letters (France, 2018). Some of her poems have been translated into several languages and published in more than 200 international anthologies, magazines and newspapers. She speaks French, English, Italian and Spanish.

The Sower's Ink of Hope

Tactile voices
Bearers of dreams
Fraction - link
The silence.
Cradle semblants
Ebony - ivory
In unison
Of our time.

Words wrap
The wings of the wind;
Inalienable right,
Universal and intrinsic
Of people.
Dreams inundate words,
Evoke consciences
Without disparity of races.
Sower's ink of hope,
Tolerance and love
Living blood in the marble of life;
As warm breeze sketching
Utopian pilasters,
Aromatic polyphonic incenses,
Seeking transcendence
In the cavities of memory.

Monsif Beroual is an internationally renowned poet from Morocco. He has received multiple awards, including The World Icon of Literature of the National Academy of Arts and Culture (India, 2020) and The Pablo Neruda Medal (2017). He is the Youth Ambassador of Morocco for Inner Child Press International. He is the founder and president of Morocco's ARTUNITED Association and the administrator of the Feelings International Artists Society. Monsif's poems have been translated into several languages, including Spanish, French, Chinese, Polish, Arabic, Romanian, Italian and Taiwanese. His work appeared in several international journals and in over 200 global anthologies.

The Realistic and Idealistic Ink

Am that human
That been lost
On the rods of life
To be a dreamer and seeker
For humanity wish,
A philosophy knowledge that teaches me
To be wise,
A letter of God that shows me the light
The light in every human into this world.
A dreamer of peace days,
A dreamer for better days
Where no wars exist,
Where all are the same,
Where you can find the joy without pain.

A better tomorrow without chains
When the walls remind you
Of incredible days,
When the presidents forgot the chess game
And policy become just in past lands
When you see human beings together
United as nations states,
No greed among those hearts
Or selfish kills that love,
When love can heal all historical tears.
When together we can forgive for a better tomorrow,
To set harmony within our souls.
A better tomorrow, when we let our heart
Speaks for love sake.
When we remember our history scars
The scar of holocaust crime,
The scar of all wars,
That human´s hand commit once
To apologize and forgive.
For a better tomorrow we can start.
Am that human who forgive
And forgot about past,
To start new days without hate.

Tyran Prizren Spahiu was born in 1954 in Kosovo. He graduated from Prishtina University with a degree in English Language and Literature. He received "The Poet of the Year" award in Pegasus, Albania. He has a novel in two volumes, *Never Back Again! – Novel MORT* and *Novel Silhouette*, and sixteen poetry books to his credit. In addition, he has authored and published the *Dream Language English Grammar-Visual English Dictionary*.

Finally, Dear Friends . . . Smiles the Future Happiness!

Being invited to join the caravan of happiness
under the blue sky of the WORLD poetry PEARLS
excited, warmly welcomed
gathered are many Nobles of the Words.

Written poems of future are so powerful
carved by the real masters of satisfaction
being followed by the sounds of guitar
followed by the steps of Argentine Tango
daffodils blossoms
peacocks boost impressively its colorful plumage
voices as midnight melodies are spread beyond the nightfall.

Please
let me be allowed to go forward to my world
would like to find peace, friendship, kindness
they are there, writers, artists, they will make me happy
with them I want to share forthcoming times
tomorrow being back home
coffee-smoking will welcome
evening brings freshness
poems flourish
easily managing to find topics that poets never miss
I feel joyfulness
smell of ink excites me
darkness slowly covers surroundings
orgy drinks of letters are poured on paper
happily breathing in the nest of JOYFULNESS.

Born and raised in India, Iram Fatima 'Ashi' is a nonresident Indian living in Saudi Arabia. Her undergraduate and graduate studies focused on English. She has been writing since the age of 13 in Hindi, Urdu, and English. She is currently the Editor-in-Chief for *Reflection* (e-zine), and is a member of the Editorial Executive Sub-Committee of the *VIEW* (print journal). Her writings appeared in 50 international anthologies, one poetry book and one novel. Her literary work has been published in magazines and newspapers in India, Canada and the US. She received an Aagman Gourav award in 2015, 2016 and 2017.

The Traveler

I am a traveler, started my journey since I was born,
I am desirous to explore the whole world and universe,
All deep depths, darkness and highness of the heights,
I want to travel to discover all the fascinating horizons.

I had reached the peaks of mountains,
To feel like a king who sees everything from heights,
Tiny small helpless creatures are visible from there,
But a view to valley horrified me by the fear of fall.

I went to the sea to play with sea waves,
To float carefree in the depth of the sea,
To discover beauty to snatch pearls for me,
Being lost in the deep dark sea again horrified me.

I explored dense vegetation dominated by trees,
Deep, dark, silent, lonesome and horrifying jungles,
Only breeze and bird's chirping were breaking the silence,
The wildness of that mystified me and arouses my inner fears.

At this moment I realized, I have to change my path,
Outer universe to deep inside my own self,
To fight with my own insecurities and fears,
The world is beautiful if I travel with the beauty of my own.

Equipped with a keen interest in history and archaeology, Shubha Khandekar is the author-illustrator of *ArchaeoGiri – A Bridge Between the Archaeologist and the Common Man*, an infotainment book on Indian archaeology. She worked as a journalist and communications consultant, and writes poetry in Marathi and English. Her poems have been included in *Amaravati poetic Prism*.

Wheels

Eons ago, it seems
Were they hallucinations, nightmares, dreams?
I flocked with silently sweating cadavers, robots, morons, puppets . . .
Buried into serpentine coffins, bursting at the seams
Yet rumbling, thundering, rolling atop
Inexorable wheels in an ephemeral touch-n-go, kiss-n-go, kick-n-go rendezvous with
The down trodden, stoic, morbid track
From one graveyard to another, and back.

Yesterday, I reckon, with the setting sun
The wheels fell silent, the wheel took a turn.
I have two of them, my very own, squeezed into my tiny kitchen
From tomorrow they will guide me, glide me
Past the jasmines, the sparrows, the diving kingfisher, the road-crossing chicken
To where I earn my bread.
And when they bring me back through the polychrome dusk
I shall inhale the breeze, squat over the doorstep, and with unfettered passion
Shower kisses on
My seldom held, though beheld often
Hypnotic companion
My mouth-organ.

K. Pankajam, a retired Finance DM, is a bilingual poet and novelist from Chennai, India. Her several poems, book reviews and articles appeared in national and international journals. She has twenty-two books to her credit, including thirteen books of poems, a translation of poetry in French and three fictions in English. *Femininity Poetic Endeavours*, *History of Contemporary Indian English Poetry* and *An Appraisal and Socio-Cultural Transition in Modern Indian English Writing & Translation*, literary critique books, discuss her work in detail. She received many prizes for her poems and short stories, such as the 2019 Rock Pebbles National Literary Award.

An Orchestra

Breeze blows music
sifts itself
through the bamboo shoots.
While trees rustle their harps,
the earth starts to sing.
Watching the leaves playful
tufted feathers of thistles
take to dancing.
In the ensemble
ambiance exulted.
A conglomeration
Symphony perfect.
I realize
I have become
a song in the concert.

Gita Bharath describes herself as a Tamilian brought up in North India. After teaching middle school for 5 years and working in banking for 34 years, she is now a busier-than-ever grandmother. She lives with her husband in Chennai and is a kolam & crossword aficionado. She loves to travel. Being blessed with an extended family, active in many fields – services, business, performing and martial arts, has broadened her outlook. Her poems deal with everyday events from different perspectives. Her six-section first book, *SVARA* mirrors 300 thought-provoking and humorous poems. Some of her work has appeared in Indian anthologies.

gitabharath@Wordpress.com

Hope

What is hope but the belief
That the sun will rise tomorrow
What is belief but a conviction
That joy triumphs over sorrow?

When the first frightened fish crawled out
From his crowded ocean home
Didn't he hope for a better life,
Look how far he's come!

The ape left his comfort zone, the tree,
To peer uneasily over the tall grass,
Did he imagine his descendants
Would dominate the world en masse?

The Romans were unchallenged
They regressed into decadence,
Too much coziness and comfort
Lead to stagnant complacence.

Every crisis is a catalyst for change
And change must be embraced
We must improve, learn from the past
For we were born to evolve apace.

Annapurna Sharma A. is Deputy Chief Editor of the literary e-journal *Muse India*. Her work has appeared in *Westward Quarterly, Mad Swirl, Spark, Destine Literare, Reader's Digest, Women's Era, Assam Tribune,* and *Active Muse*. She contributes to *Muse India* and the *Triveni Journal* with her book reviews. A nutritionist by profession but a writer at heart, her maiden poetry book, *Melodic Melange* was recognized with an award for excellence (2019, Pulitzer Books). One of her poems was shortlisted for the All India Poetry Competition, conducted by The Poetry Society of India in 2017.

Soulmates

My heart skipped a beat
When the southern winds filled my pen
Ichor soaking my innards
The pages fluttered past
A gush of night jasmine
The letters, the verse, the stanza
Wrapped me in gossamer folds
And rapturous silence

I don't remember when this journey began
Of gathering words and phrases
In my bosom
Packing them in topsoil
In a glass jar
And placing them on the window sill
To pullulate

One might wonder - why the glass jar?
So I transcend, to be a part of that germ
My germ –
Perspiring and blossoming
Why the window sill?
So I could hear the heavenly coo-coo of my cuckoo
Before the rain showers

When rainbow splashes myriad hues
On my poesy
When I, a poet
Tender and touching
At that midnight hour
Witness perfect happiness
Verselets are my aphrodisiac

The Conscious Poets

When Rumi and Shams met
. . . those who love with heart and soul
There is no such thing as separation . . .
I penned a serif . . .

The Heart of a Poet

Sumita Dutta Shoam is the founder of Adisakrit, a publishing house that takes pride in producing books in a variety of genres. She enjoys the most creative mediums of expression. She has a degree in Fine Arts and loves photography. She is fluent in English, Hindi, spoken Bengali, and has learnt rudimentary French. She loves to explore places and cultures, and has been lucky enough to travel to twenty-two countries. Her work is available on several websites, and some of her poems have appeared in print anthologies. *The Heart of Donna Rai* is her debut novel.

I Dream

I dream
A boundaryless world—
Earthlings
traveling freely
anywhere
On Earth
as birth right.
Mother Earth's children
All living creatures—
siblings.
Our family
living in harmony.
Plants in my garden
lovingly wrap tendrils
around my lingering fingers.
Birds hop into my yard
stalking food with righteous
circumspection
despite grains placed for them.
They are as welcome
as the colourful butterflies
meandering in
to gladden my heart,
if only they knew.
It's the mischief
they've caused—
tipped pots,
plants pecked to death . . .
Yes, wariness comes
from the knowledge
of mischievous instincts.
But their hearts are pure,
they are welcome
to my home.
I dream

The Heart of a Poet

I was welcome
to explore alpine forests
meander into ancient castles
sit in ancient houses of God
sail the Bosporus, Nile, Altana . . .
clamber over Rockies, Andes, Pyrenees . . .
ride into deserts—Tanami, Kalahari, Atacama . . .
Live my colourful motherland
in all her glory
one day
post COVID-19 . . .

Ndaba Sibanda is the author of *Notes, Themes, Things and Other Things*; *The Gushungo Way*; *Sleeping Rivers*; *Love O'clock*; *The Dead Must Be Sobbing*; *Football of Fools*; *Cutting-edge Cache*; *Of the Saliva and the Tongue*; *When Inspiration Sings In Silence*; *The Way Forward*; *The Ndaba Jamela*, and *Collections and Poetry Pharmacy*. Sibanda is a 2019 Pushcart nominee.

The Pedagogy of Humanity, Humility and Hope

If there is a lesson to be learnt from the COVID-19 pandemic
Then it is that humanity is one, and must always be human-centric

A world that treasures love will build beautiful bridges of cooperation
And seek to get rid of greed and animosities, and redefine civilization

Prioritize people`s welfare, not warfare, neither competition nor extinction
It is time to uplift spirits with our abilities to move to correction, elevation!

Let the tomorrow be a bastion of robust health systems across the entire globe
Clean air, a roof, a decent meal, healthcare for all, should be our pleased probe

Resurrection of lost species and the creation of artificial life through technology
Is not worth it if the protection of the natural world is not part of the pedagogy

Gobinda Biswas, whose literary language is English, has composed 400 poems since 2013. He has 3 poetry books to his credit, *The Sunny Poems*, *The Universal Poems* and *The Eternal Poems*. The first two were published in 2017 by Progressive Publishers in Kolkata, and the 3rd, by Authors Press in New Delhi in 2019. His 4th poetry book is pending publication. He participated in many international poetry festivals, and his poems appeared in numerous anthologies, magazines and e-zines across the world. His poetry readings are available on his You Tube Channel and on his website.

www.gobindabiswas.com

We Won't Fear

We won't fear, we won't fear, oh my dears,
We have conquered so many fatal fears.
We were born under the horrible open sky
Though anxious, we didn't surrender thereby.

We fought utmost against the cruel Nature,
She couldn't suppress us with severe torture.
Nature always stood nearby but to crucify,
She tried her best but we did not really die.

She sent earth-quake, drought, flood, famine,
We suffered a lot but revived afresh again.
Even then we loved a firefly and a butterfly,
To overcome all dangers, we fought like a Samurai.

We fought against enemies in thousands of battles,
But we survived from the jaws of crocodiles.
Like the dinosaurs here we would not die,
We are immortal; with death we can vie.

We won't be abolished, we are the Phoenix,
We'll resurrect, we'll resurrect like the Christ.
Come Corona, come Death, we would not cry,
We won't fear, we won't fear, we're truly so spry.

The Conscious Poets

Yuan Changming published monographs on translation before leaving China. With a Canadian Ph.D. in English, he currently edits *Poetry Pacific* with Allen Qing Yuan in Vancouver. 1709 distinctions across 45 countries, excluding ten Pushcart nominations, eight chapbooks, the Jodi Stutz Award in Poetry (2020), and inclusion in *Best of the Best Canadian Poetry* (2008-17) and *BestNewPoemsOnline.com*, represent the wide-spread recognition of his literary work.

Birds of Varied Feathers: A Neo-Confucian Call

Come, come, come on
You *peng* from the Zhuangzian northern twilight
You swan from the Horacean meadows
You pheasant from under Li Bo's cold moon
You oriole from Dufu's green willow
You dove from the Dantean inferno
You phoenix from Shakespeare's urn
You swallow from the Goethe oak or
The Nerudan dense blue air, you cuckoo
From the Wordsworthian vale, you albatross
From the Coleridgean fog, you nightingale
From the Keatsian plum tree, you skylark
Form the Shalleyean heaven, you owl
From under the Baudelairen overhanging years
You unnamed creature from the Pushkinian alien lands
You raven from near Poe's chamber door
You parrot from the Tagorean topmost twig
And you crow from among my cawing words

Come, come on, all of you, more than 100 kinds of
Birds from every time spot or spot moment

Come, with your light but strong skeletons
Come, with your toothless but hardened beaks
Come, with your colored feathers, and flap your wings
Against Su dongpo's painting brush strokes

Come, all you free spirits of nature
With your powerful wings of hope
Come on, each and every one of you
Through the suffocating storms of yesterday
Through the deafening darkness of tonight

Let's join one another and flock together
High, higher up above the rainbows
Towards Gaxyland, the harmonious world of tomorrow

Welkin Siskin is a writer whose poems have been published in several anthologies. He has authored a book of poetry, *Ten Worlds: A Collection of Poems* (Inner Child Press International, September 15, 2019). He lives in Washington.

Questing After Truth

We sing our lullabies
To the stardust
And plant our hearts
To kiss the moon.
We sow the light of hope
Across a prism,
Distance to the furthest
To gather testament of life,
To find a gospel of truth.
We sing psalms of life thus:
Hungered after things unknown,
Leaving behind void souls, astray
And stark unbeknownst, of our existence.

Ashrit Mohapatra is a college student from Odisha, India with a passion for writing poetry.

My Dream

My dream is my fashion
Comes every day
Tells me about love
Laughing likely gay.

My dream is my fashion
Brings different stage
Often fear often smile
And enjoy myself gaze.

My dream is my fashion
Shows me luxury thing
My passion happily dances
Even I am the king.

My dream is my fashion
Learn me like a friend
Living from my childhood
That is never end.

A nurse by profession, Luzviminda G. Rivera is a prize-winning author. She is a researcher with multiple awards, an international reviewer of research journals and an inspirational poet from the Philippines. She speaks six languages fluently. She is also a licensed teacher, having completed her post-graduate courses with recognition for "Academic Excellence". [. . .] She has authored *A Gift*, *A Gift II* and *Crossroads: A Poet's Life Journey* (an anthology). Currently, she is a moderator for the Philippines office of "Motivational Strips" and one of the editors of the India-based e-zine, "Bharath Vision".

A New Beginning

Every morning that brings new life
Is a new beginning:
To shine like the sunrise
To smell the aroma of fragrant flower
To feel the touch of the billowing breeze
To hear the rustling leaves of the trees
To see the refreshing view of clouds
To witness the vibrant colors of rainbows

Above all
A new beginning:

To treasure our moment on earth
To let go of the things that belong to the earth
To focus on what counts most
In the end.

The Conscious Poets

Nutan Sarawagi is from Mumbai, India. Poetry is her passion. She loves to colour words in verse. She has a master's degree in Education and is a designer by profession. She writes mainly on women and children. She feels very strongly about women's issues and the children of war. She wishes she could set the world right for them. She writes in English and Hindi.

A Poet's Fight to Live

a poet's fight to live his life
not the way the world wants him to live
but the way he wants to in his strife
he knows no other way in his life
his life is to fight for others
he knows no other way of life
help him let him live his way

to fight again his fight with him his own way
cause if nothing is left within him to fight
he will die within, perishing in . . . within him his fight
and when all fight will die within him that day
everything will die within us that day
that day the world will die in itself
that day it will end
it will be the world's end that day

when birds in the world will not sing
when hope will not live for another day
to live in its hope for another day
let all hope live for that day
when all poets will live in the hope of that day to stay
when all voices will together be sung
in a hope together . . . together will be rung
bringing in the hope of a new hope
to rejoice in the hope that day
when everybody will love
in the hope of that day
when all hope will be one
in that hope we will live for that day
in our hope we will celebrate that day

when there will be nothing to fear
no people no war no hate
only peace to love . . . in peace no hate
that day when people in the world
will unite as one
from heaven will descend all peace
in peace to be one

The Conscious Poets

there will be no fights left in us that day
we will be waiting in life's heaven to fight our way
in heaven
to be in heaven as in one
when peace will descend on heaven
on earth we will be one
no more wars only love to be won
no wars only love to be won . . . only love to be won . . . only love . . .
only love . . . only love to be won

in peace we lie
in love we have our war of peace
we have just won to fight ourselves our love apiece
to find peace in our war against love and peace
we have won . . . we have won

we now rest in peace our own peace we are at last one
to be in peace with peace we have won
we are in peace with ourselves
now nobody can fight us in our war of peace
we have already won

to fight ourselves in our peace
we now lie defeated
in our defeat to defeat war we are one we will always be one . . .
nothing is lost we have forever won

in our mission to fight war we have won only won
let us end this war against peace
one day to find peace and peace within us to stay
for we are peace

let us bring heaven in peace to this day
when some of it might trickle down to earth
on its way
and the earth will shine in peace
and peace will shine
in its own way
for it has come to stay on earth
on earth in its own way
and all the dead who were killed in war

The Heart of a Poet

rise and celebrate peace with us . . . in peace
we will all rise . . . to celebrate peace which left us one day
and now has come to stay
with us forever now it is to stay
we will never let this peace go away
it is our peace we love it
in which we want to live
to be ours in it to never ever let it go away
we are the holders of peace in us it has come to reside
nobody can now take it away from us
it is now for us in it to abide
in it we live in it we die
it is ours in it to live or to die
take it away and there is nothing left
to live in peace we live and in peace we die

it's ours to choose in it to live or die

let that day come when we have nothing to choose
in our choice for peace there is nothing left to choose
only peace only peace we live for that day
when peace will fall from heaven like hail
on that day in heaven we will hail
almighty will be one
in peace we will rise from heaven
God will be one

and all Gods will come in us to stay
we will be God's heaven on that day
when even God will rise and salute us
from heaven and let us have his way

when the earth will be heaven heaven all the way
when we will be heaven on earth there will be no heaven left to stay
on earth there will be heaven all heaven along the way

the streets will be strewed with love
and heaven will shower more love from above
and heaven will come to earth to stay . . . to stay
with us to never go away
in heaven we will live in heaven we will sigh

when pavements will be paved with love all the way
we will be heaven

and heaven will have come with us to stay
in heaven we will all stay

only heaven only heaven stretching for miles and miles
nothing else will be seen as it stretches to heaven all the way
in this heaven to find our heaven we lie for that day
when we will all be one to live
in our heaven of our heaven to live for that day
in peace in peace strewed along heavens path
stretching to the earth in pavements lit with love
only peace, peace stretching for miles along the way

The Heart of a Poet

A risk manager by profession with a passion for writing poetry, K. Radhakrishnan lives in Bhopal, India. He has four poetry books to his credit, *Reflection of Soul* (Lulu Press, USA), *Eruption of Bottled Up Emotions* (Vishwabharati Research Centre), *Moods in Motion* and *Dazzling Dance of Poesy* (both published by the Aabs Publication House in Kolkata). He has contributed to many international poetry anthologies with his poems. Radhakrishnan has won many poetry contests and his poems are regularly featured on international poetry sites, such as Destiny Poets UK, ATUNIS Poetry and Spillwords Press.

A Futuristic Vision

With these heavenly pair of lenses,
I envision world of accord and consensus,
A vision to knock down man made fences,
To regain our lost senses.

A vision to build bridges to connect hearts,
To free the humanity tied up in knots,
I am on a mission to connect the dots,
And to fill up our insecure spots.

While traversing through life's ridges,
I have the vision to round off uneven edges,
Cementing it with love, leaving no glitches,
And fill the life with love centered sketches.

A vision to create a word of harmony,
Eyes visualize concept of universal family,
Out on a mission to turn this in to a reality,
To conquer with love, the galaxy.

One love, and one world is the desire of heart,
Together as one, we have to make a sincere start,
In this mission, we all have to play our part,
Then this vision will turn out so smart.

A world where all make honest earning,
Where all follow the things they are learning,
To create world where love's light is burning,
My dream, my vision and my yearning.

To see world where no one dies of starvation,
To create an order devoid of destruction,
I envision the world where all children get education,
Where there is no racial discrimination.

pages are blank and it is for us to write story,
 Future is what we make of it, let us turn it in to glory,
Have the ambition to climb life's highest story,
Vision and unhampered mission are the mantras of victory.

The Heart of a Poet

Smruti Ranjan Mohanty, Finance Officer in the Government of Odisha, is from Padmapur. He is a multilingual poet, writer and an essayist. His work has appeared in numerous newspapers, in more than 200 national and international anthologies, print and online magazines and journals, including Atunis poetry.com, Our Poetry Archive, poemhunter.com, GloMag, Setu, *The Year of the Poet* (USA), and Youtube. He writes extensively on life and its intricacies. He was a featured poet of the PENTASI B World Friendship Poetry and *The Year of the Poet*. His 10 poem collections [. . .] are in press.

Website-smrutiweb.wordpress.com

smrutitanuja.blogspot.com

Life Divine

Life is as simple as the clear blue sky
We make it hazy
Life is living in reality
We make it worst of a mirage
Life is not about accumulating assets
That boomerang at you
Turn into liabilities at a later stage
It is not about building relationships
That strongly bind you to the world
Become the cause of your sorrow and misery

Life is not about carrying a heavy load
Feeling breathless under its pressure
Ultimately succumbing to it sooner or later
The more you carry the more you worry
Less the luggage better the journey
Faster the movement
Life is freedom
That makes you a free bird in the open sky
Going higher and higher searching the elixir

Life is not an endless strife
To go-ahead of others
It is an opportunity to look at your self
And take rapid strides towards the destination
You hold high

Life is not about laurels and accolades
Clapping and cheers
Parade of ego, selfishness and vanity
It is a vow divine
To know, by knowing which
You do not need to know anything

The Heart of a Poet

Life is not about adding years
It is more about adding beauty and grace
Knowledge and wisdom
And living with a purpose

No matter live in the world
But never let the world live in you
That is the cause of your bondage
And the biggest tragedy of life
If you can go beyond it
Your life will be life divine

The Conscious Poets

From Chennai, India, Vidya Shankar is a poet, writer, English teacher, motivational speaker, yoga enthusiast, an editor and an exponent of mindful mandalas. She has authored two poetry books, *The Flautist of Brindaranyam* and *The Rise of Yogamaya*, and is the recipient of numerous literary awards and recognitions. She has been on the editorial board of three anthologies. A "book" with the Human Library, Shankar uses the power of words to create awareness about mental health and other oppressing issues of an outdated society.

Unbounded Crescendo

The painting was huge
Occupying the almost entire wall
Behind the reception desk
Of the resort hotel I was checking into.
Overwhelmed, I stood as if in trance
My fascination not for the immensity
Of the painting, but for the painting itself.
It was a picture of a cage
Gilded, golden, glamorous
Its door open but just enough
Through which were flying out, soaring to freedom
Caged birds.

I saw myself there, as one among them
A caged bird
'With clipped wings and tied feet
As Maya's birds were
And though I didn't open my throat to sing
I stood not, unlike them, on a grave of dreams'*
For, I dared to dream and believed it too
Of a life in the skies
Out and beyond the gilded bonds
So I lived in trust, finding strength
In patient faith and the truth of my breath
Knowing that one day someone would come along
To open the door, maybe not wide, but just enough
For me to find my way, out and away
From the claustrophobic constriction
Of age-old metallic patterns
Out and away, flying on a song.

The retreat in the resort was dreamlike —
Four days of unrestrained holidaying
From the self I had always been expected
To live by
Taught me that my existence in bondage
Was of my own making.
Four days of unbridled existence spent
I set back to where I belonged

The Conscious Poets

To don once again the hood I was expected
To wear.
At the airport, a picture greeted me —
Un-caged birds, wings spread wide
Frolicking and rollicking among buoyant clouds
A birdsong of sunshine
Wafting among lush green treetops —
I saw myself there, a free bird
I knew then what I wanted, what I had to do
I knew then that I did not have to wait
For a someone to un-cage me
I discarded with decisive flourish
The cowering hood I was expected to wear
Untied my feet, flicked the latch open
And stepped out of the claustrophobic cage
Gilded, golden, glamorous though it was
I didn't need it anymore
My clipped wings fell, new powerful ones
Sprouting in its stead, full of colour
I flapped my wings and took off
Sweeping and soaring to the skies and beyond
The heady feeling of liberation
Opened up my choked throat
And I sang out loud and lilting, my lyrical birdsong
A fitting crescendo of my unbounded ascension.

*With clipped wings and tied feet [. . .] a grave of dreams: A reference to Maya Angelou's poem "Caged Bird".

The Heart of a Poet

From the state of Odisha in India, Dr. Sudarsan Sahu is a hydrogeologist by profession and works as a scientist in the Central Ground Water Board, a department under the Ministry of Jal Shakti in the Government of India. Though he has excelled in his field of research with several publications, he bears a poetic bent of mind from his childhood. He is a trilingual poet and writes on issues related to the climate and ecology and on social themes in Oriya, Hindi and English.

I Will Be Fearless Again

I will be fearless again, in my mother's lap
When,
she will put a smile in her face
again,
looking at me, with that affection and charm
the morbid and agonizing days, will go for ever
the despondent soul, will be rhapsodic, lively
waking up, to the sweet call, of my mother
in the morning symphony, and the chorus of birds
when, the golden rays of sun
will sow new hopes, in the yards and streets
and in every step that I count, like a butterfly
damn sure!
I will be fearless again, in my mother's lap

My heart will be chilled again, in tranquility and peace
when,
the magical touch of my mother will slide past
again,
caressing my face, hair and the inner spirit,
in gusts of breeze over the beaches and lofty woods
where, I will be playful again, with the bounties of life
looking at the divine beauty of my mother
and by adding feathers of her love in my wings
will write new anecdotes of life
on the flower petals and on the wet sand at seashore
getting an adoring hug of my mother again
damn sure!
my heart will be chilled again, in tranquility and peace

The Heart of a Poet

Canzoni del Vederdi Sera (Friday Night Songs) is John Eliot's newest collection to be published on July 15, 2020 by Mosaïque Press. It is a collection of 40 poems that represents John's work from the 1970s to the present, selected by John and his editor, Paola Fornari. The book is a collaboration between the poet and the talented young translators, Alessia Calabrese, Sara Pallante, Alessandro Pinto and Mariagrazia Poppiti. John's other collections, also from Mosaique Press, are *Ssh* (2014), *Don't Go* (2016) and *Turn on the Dark* (2018).

I Will Breathe

in anticipation
waiting upon dawn
where I can draw
a different breath

The Heart of a Poet

Alicja Maria Kuberska from Poland is an award-winning poet, a novelist, journalist and an editor. She is a member of the Polish Writers Association in Warsaw, Poland and the IWA Bogdani in Albania. She is also a member of the directors' board of the Soflay Literature Foundation and Our Poetry Archive (India), and Cultural Ambassador for Poland (Inner Child Press International, USA).

A Philosopher and a Poet

They met between heaven and earth
at the place where time and matter are irrelevant,
at a higher level of abstraction.
They overcame the barriers of the real world.

He brought a white canvas and philosophical maxims.
She brought the paint brushes
and a handful of dreams in words.
They painted the picture in many shades of blue.
They poured their thoughts and feelings into the ether.

He sketched the outlines of life with a bold navy-blue line.
She filled the background with gentle azure brushes.
Together they added a few colorful spots of astonishment.
His eyes are hazel and hers are green

Fahredin Shehu, born in Rahovec, Kosova, is a 2017 Pulitzer Poetry Prize nominee and the recipient of numerous prestigious poetry awards. He graduated from Prishtina University with a degree in Oriental Studies, and is a certified expert in adult learning on the platforms of capacity building, training, coaching, mentoring and facilitating. He has eight books to his credit, *The Pen*, *Dismantling Hate*, *Crystalline Echoes*, *Pleroma's Dew*, *Maelstrom*, *Bonds*, *Neon Child* and *HERENOW*. Shehu's poems have been translated into a large number of languages. Presently, he operates as an independent scholar in the fields of World Spiritual Heritage and Sacral Esthetics.

The Velvet Notebook

On the aquamarine velvet notebook
a heavy Pen writes harshly
with the blood instead of ink and
the straight letters for the curved world

The Heart of a Poet

Preety Sengupta is a poet, fiction-writer and an essayist. She is from India, and has been living in New York for many years. She writes in English as well as in her mother tongue. Her books have received many prizes and awards. Her work is included in several anthologies in India and in the USA.

Many Brave Tales

This blade of grass is strong.
I know.
I have seen it last through
Last year's snow.
I have seen it
Come out of the frigidity all around
– Slowly, but surely –
All of its two-inch-tall slender frame,
Still pale green,
Standing out straight, but not stiff,
Confident, but not arrogant.

These attributes are in its genes
–to be sinuous and strong,
–to be gracious and grand.
Being quiet is not being incapable,
Being kind is not being weak.

Time will tell its many brave tales.
The paleness will soon transform into
Fully bloomed splendor.
Its tender heart will swell again,
Nourished by solidarity.
New warmth will flow in its veins
Like summer rain on expectant earth.

Ahila is a writer and an artist (fine arts). She works as a Counselling Psychologist in Coimbatore, India. Her literary work appears in English and Tamil. She has authored and published ten books – four poetry collections, two non-fictions, a novella and two short story collections in Tamil and one poetry collection in English.

Opened

'Opened', named the warm gardens!
'Opened', smiled the lonely beaches!
'Opened', cried the spicy restaurants!

Butterflies, birds and Begonias
in full bloom and bright!
Elephants, civic cats, deer
on the road, unwind them leisurely
Monkeys talked aloud with trees,
'So, this world is ours'

Humans are let out of their houses
for a few hours to cool off, they
Can walk softly, so not to
rupture the earth
Can mumble softly, so not to
disturb the wind
Can breathe still, so not to
trouble the blossom

Opened and Fresh
So humans started to believe
'This world is natural'

The Heart of a Poet

Claudia Piccinno, teacher and poet, is the Continental Director of the World Poetry Festival for Europe. She has received multiple awards for her poems and translations. She has 36 multi-lingual poetry books to her credit.

White flag

Climbing to the sky
I wave a white banner
to greet those who have undertaken
a single journey.
Geraniums bloomed;
they tell me that life goes on,
that I have to ignore the fear
if I want to stay.
So I'm looking for the blue of the day
in order to start again . . .

The Heart of a Poet

Maryam Abbasi is a poet of Indian origin. An academic by profession, she took to writing professionally 3 years ago. Her poems have been published internationally and nationally since then. Being an ardent reader, she has always been fascinated by words, and it was due to this love that she started penning her own thoughts secretly onto her Twitter page. It has been quite a journey for her, from her words being kept anonymously to her own acknowledgement of them with her name.

A Stretch Across the Sky: Ghar*

And hurry past home,
O, little child of my own.
Across the street,
cross all the red lights,
Run away from a few.
On your way back home,
Remember to count your steps too.
Feel the earth,
Drink the sky,
Let your head run wild,
Let that smile of yours shine,
Step 1
Step 2
It has been a long way back home.
And in these moments,
When you're free,
Dance a step or a two,
Step 1
Step 2
Remember to let little things go.
You have beauty in your heart,
And we need no more,
Stars, gold or sin,
You are more than those.
Let the world live its life
You, on your own are doing nice.
O, sweet little child of mine
I am glad, you are finally learning to smell like home.

*Ghar: The Urdu word for "home"

Andrew Scott is a native of Fredericton, NB. During his time as an active poet, he has taken the time to speak in front of classrooms, judge poetry competitions and author over 200 hundred writings. His work has been published worldwide in literary books, including *The Art of Being Human*, *Battered Shadows* and *The Broken Ones*. Scott has five poetry books to his credit, *Snake with A Flower*, *The Phoenix Has Risen*, *The Path*, *The Storm Is Coming* and *Searching*. He has also authored one book of photography, *Through My Eyes*.

Stronger Together

Know that inside you are hurting
the mind is clouded and confused
everything is making you feel alone
searching for answers as to why
without a clear tunnel to go

There are people out everywhere
feeling the same conflicted emotions
that is hitting you and your heart

As we walk through this with each other
breathe in, taste how precious it all is
there is a new sky every day
look up, it is beautiful
even when the look is grey

Take a hand, hold it together
all of us, as one, so we all can see
feel the strength of us, lifting
can walk along, struggle by struggle
overcoming all as we are stronger together

The Heart of a Poet

Dr. Paramita Mukherjee Mullick is a scientist by education, educator by profession and a poet by passion. She has published five books. She is the founder and president of the Mumbai Chapter of the Intercultural Poetry and Performance Library. Some of her poems have been translated into 31 languages. Her poetry has appeared in more than 250 national and international publications. She has been blessed with numerous awards for her poetry, including the Gold Rose from Argentina for promoting literature and culture. She lives in Mumbai, India.

Rainbow Clouds

The sky was overcast with dark clouds.
There was silence all around.
Not a leaf shivered, not a soul stirred.
It was an unknown fear.

The roads were empty.
Each was fearful about the other.
Quarantined and isolated at home.
Each heart beat with trepidation.

Suddenly they looked out.
There was light and light all around.
The birds twittered, oh the wondrous sound!
The sky was filled with rainbow clouds.

Colours, colours everywhere.
Nature had painted the clouds with a brush.
The multi-hues brought happiness in a flash.
The colours washed away all fear and doubt.

The rainbow clouds were the sentinels of happiness.
Lockdown was no more and all could meet again.
Disease and dread vanished and waned.
Uncertainties became history and the world came alive.

The Heart of a Poet

Eden Soriano Trinidad hails from the Philippines. She is a poet, translator, and an entrepreneur. She has translated 4 epic books of famous international authors into Filipino. Her poetry has been translated into various languages. Her love-poems are featured on full page in the weekend issue of *Văn Nghệ* (a Haiphong newspaper), *Nhật Lệ Vietnam* (a literary magazine), *Science Herald* (the Chinese national newspaper), and the *First World Daily Poetry in Macao and Weixin*. The University of the Philippines Institute of the Philippines Creative Writing Freelipiniana Online Library published five of her books.

The Parlance of a Poet

We are a soul tandem
that will sprinkle glimpses of truths
upon the great walls
of dispassion and disillusioned souls

We are the sun and earth
so distant yet so near
tandem to enkindle life
black nights follow morning delights

How many applauses our poems offer?
To brim hopes
that will partake sunbeams
to the darkened spirit of human souls

We are lockdown but not knockdown
believing when we unite we will stand
we are enclosed while the creatures are free
we may never be what we used to be

But we are tandem of repertoire
to enshrine then sprinkle candor
implore peaceful coexistence
as the heart is the parlance of a poet.

The Heart of a Poet

Anna Nicole D. Velez is 19 years old and a proud Filipino citizen. She aspires to become a "Voice" – a voice of truth, a voice of freedom, a voice of faith and a voice of empowerment.

Just Breathe

When all feels sinking deep
And fear comes knocking down your feet
Packed with an ice-cold heart and dreams
Pause for a second
Live by what you feel
Just breathe

Hold all the black and blues
Look over thy wounds
Listen to the tune
Sniff the aroma of truth
Fall in love first with its roots
For someday you'll see its growing fruits

Life will not breathe
Without an oxygen of grief
For it is only through oceans deep
Mountains high and valleys low
Where we can find His resting grace and peace

When eyes are shut
Feeling lost
And about to die
There comes a new life
From a Father who keeps on holding our breath

His love never fails
And never changes . . .

So, continue to breathe

Please, just breathe . . .

The Heart of a Poet

Awatef El Idrissi Boukhris is a Moroccan poet and novelist. She studied in an interpreters' school in Mons, Belgium, and is now working as a teacher of English. She has four poetry collections to her credit – two in English and two in French, and a novel in French. She also writes stories for the youth in French and English. In addition to her creative writing endeavors, she has been a cultural correspondent for a local paper for six years where her poems and articles were published. She has contributed to many French and English anthologies with her literary work.

Dare to Dream

Dare to fly
On the wings of the wind
Hug the sun
Caress the moon
Float in clouds of bounty
Wash in streams of light
Purify your soul
And pray in the temple of peace

Dare to swim
In rivers of love
Mercy and compassion
Open your heart
To lodge every soul
Be the balm
To every wound
And to all the desperate in the world
Dare to sleep
On mountain tops
Having for bed the grass
And for blanket the stars
Quench your thirst
From the morning dew
Drink the flowers' nectar
Till inebriation

Dare to dive
In the heart of the poet
And see how wide it is
How it overflows with love
With hope and faith
For a better tomorrow
Full of happiness
And no sorrow

The Heart of a Poet

Dare to dream
Of a just world
Where all people are alike
Where there is no racism or violence
No more wars or conflicts
No more aggression or killings
Only love and charity
Kindness and empathy

The Conscious Poets

Born in 1962 in Nabeul, Tunisia, Fethi Sassi is a poet, translator, and HAIKU writer. He became passionate about poetry at the very early stages of his life. His poems have appeared in numerous journals and anthologies. He has four books to his credit, *Seed of Love* (2010), *I Dream . . . I Sign on Birds the Last Words* (2013), *Sky for a Strange Bird* (2016), and *As a Lone Rose . . . on a Chair* (2017). He is a member of The Union of the Tunisian Poets and The Literature Club of the Sousse cultural center.

A High Tree

He put a handful of soil on the whiteness,
Wet the words.
Heaved a sigh of relief,
Then drew a high tree
But! Can he call it a high tree?
He drew branches, leaves and storms,
Put the sun on the table.
Thus, it became a beautiful garden
This is a beautiful garden.
One scared leaf fell from the tree,
He drew its shadow
and cried his eyes out . . .
Then disappeared into the shadow.

Ashok Kumar is an internationally noted poet from India. He is the principal of a well-known educational institution. His poetry is of philosophical, spiritual and mystical nature. His poems have been translated and published in many languages, including Hindi, English, Spanish, French, and Greek. He holds the world-view of Aurobindo Ghosh, the Walt Whitman Professor and Dr. Nelson Mandela. He believes in non-violence and has received numerous national and international peace awards.

Hope for the Future

The wonderful world
is in the grip of world war
the peace makers;
need of the hours
Not nuclear weapons,
but only humanity can make
the whole world strong
the nation who stand for integrity
bring peace and prosperity
Peace makers who work while others
sleep with gold coins
Men are all equal to attain divine beauty
be as monk
for the welfare of humanity
They build the confidence pillars deep
And lift them to the infinite sky
Cowards weep while brave hearts
touches the height of sky
let's keep up their spirits who lose hope
during pandemic time
let's keep our promise before die

A writer, novelist, poet, researcher, historian and lecturer, Ana María Manuel Rosa is an Honorary Member of the International Arts Council; Universal Ambassador of Peace; Universal Ambassador of Culture; Literature Ambassador, and Humanitarian Ambassador of the Hospital ÁFRICA 55 project. She has 22 books to her credit and has contributed to 26 multi-lingual anthologies based in Argentina, Bolivia, Colombia, Chile, Peru, Trinidad, Albania, India, Indonesia and Taiwan. Rosa has written for international e-zines and participated in writers' meetings in different countries. She has been interviewed by different media and awarded worldwide.

"The Heart of a Poet"

Such a drop of rainwater or a great sea;
Just like a seed of a floral species
It gives beautiful flowers, fruit plantations,
Or like the shadow of a lush forest
And like forging steel with excellent
Quality to make a sharp knife and
Strong is "the heart of the poet" that with
Great imagination takes his/her pen molding
The correct words expressing his/her feelings.
Feelings and realities; leaving messages
To posterity, shaping thoughts
And ideas of the moment that reflects the heart
Of the poet in action with what happens.
Romance, youth, motherhood, family,
Friendship, work, politics ... in a simple
Paper with the ink of a pen and hand
Is perpetuated feeling; messages are made
What society would like to say. Alone
The writer and the poet put the words
Exact in poetry demanding justice.
The essence of that womb, inborn cradle
From the peaceful heart with expertise
Of the letters and the handling of the same
It is called the true heart of the poet.
Like a cry to the universe, to humanity;
All in verses with words they draw with
Simplicity is an awakening of consciences.
The poetry; an appeal to those who preach
Hate and traffic in death; trace those
Paths of love, solidarity, harmony,
Freedom, correction of behaviors because
The message is strong with a double meaning
Powerful metaphor inducing change
Of mentality awakening consciences.
Traced paths for humanity

The Conscious Poets

And bridges that unite; warding off doom
Of war, hatred and revenge.
The words sweet, loving, warm and
Sincere can mobilize the heart
Asleep to the giant evil tyrant.
Those words trace paths where not
They find obstacles; induce thinking and
To meditate; managing to extinguish destroying
Bombs, grenades, tanks and bulldozing
Trenches of war. Like a music
Conciliatory words spoken by the poet
They manage to heal fatal wounds, disappointments
And unite hearts that cry and dry tears
Running because the truth is that magic
It came, minds changed and the truth is
That it was the work of "The Heart of a Poet".

Born in Katwa and brought up in Raina, India, Dr. Debaprasanna Biswas is a Bengali poet. He is a retired Associate Professor of Mathematics and Honorary Professor at the Facility of Science in Lincoln University in Kolez, Malaysia. As a teenager, he edited a literary publication, *Banasabha*. He has received the "Best Writer of the Year 2019" award from Bangabhumi Sahitya Parishad, an esteemed literary group in Dhaka, Bangladesh. He participated as a speaker in conferences at home and abroad. He is a member of the Central Committee at the International Council of Human and Fundamental Rights in India.

The Gift of Corona

In lockdown, miles after miles
With a dreadful determination
Homeless in thousands
Walking an endless path to home.
That was a reality, as communication stopped.
A good number couldn't finish journey
For the want of food and energy.
But nothing to lose
Setting Sun awaits the next Sunrise.
The gray horizon gradually appears green
What a blue sky with white floating cottons.
Where's the suffocating air
Where's the trail of smoke from chimney
No vehicle pollution
Every nuisance has gone.
After the threat of corona.
More the lockdown declared step by step
More the world is under the process of recovery.
The boredom of class learning is gone
Dynamic improvisation of e-learning started.
New Sunshine of digitalism is peeping through the horizon.
Health consciousness grows with mask as armour
Next-gen to breath in a pollution free environment
On the theme of sanitization

The Heart of a Poet

Lily Swarn, a columnist, Peace and Humanity Ambassador for various institutions in Morocco and Ghana and an internationally acclaimed poet, has a university degree. Her poetry collection, *A Trellis of Ecstasy* was lauded by London's *Journal of Commonwealth Literature*. Reviews for her books, *The Gypsy Trail*, *Lilies of the Valley* and *History on My Plate* are widely available. She is the recipient of 45 prizes, including the Reuel International Prize for Poetry, Global Icon of Peace, Frang Bardhi (Albania), and World Icon (Peru, Venezuela and Kazakhstan). She writes in 4 languages. Her poetry has been translated into 16 languages.

A Rossini Crescendo

I walk along the sandy shores of my ephemeral being
Watching dusk seduce me with its flaming passion
I know it'll be time for pack up soon
For the countdown has started ticking on my ageing visage

I beseech the world to stop for me, my best is yet to come
Luminous layers lush with lustrous lure
Beckon me to forage for the divine sound of Anhad Nad
Beyond the dome of teal blue incandescence

It's time to give back generously to this awe-inspiring macrocosm
That made me blossom from a microcosmic cell to a thudding heart that feels and loves
It's a Rossini Crescendo moment in my tantalizing human opera
Let my open up my throat and heart to the whispering willows

Come Universe, let me absorb you in myself today
Becoming one with your healing aura
Quantum physics unraveling the magic of mystical atoms
Let me soak in the shimmer of the Parmatama
In my limping, lisping aatama

The Heart of a Poet

The author uses the word "eye" instead of the letter "I". She says it connects her deeper to the spirit of what she is writing. Her social media name at the moment is "Valerie Ames". It has been Mutha Wit Wisdom and (0) ocean 9. A mother of two grown children and a grandmother of six, she considers herself to be an eclectic expression of existence. Life, she believes, is an artistic expression.

The Heart . . . of Tomorrow . . .

It is often with a heavy heart that eye peer
Through previous past traumatic experiences
Seen through a lens of Life . . . that has been none too gentle with me
Fabricated out of ill fashioned fatalities profoundly felt

Through the shadows of the valley of death
Eye crawled . . . carrying those who came before me on my back
Always . . . more concerned for their pain than mine . . . born with silence
Weight born from the innocent purloined apportioned pounds of flesh

But lately something very profound has risen 2 the surface
Resistance . . . existing from the ancient depths of my conscious awareness
Eye no longer felt alone with my task . . . as a new collective has ascended
My heart has expanded beyond tomorrow's tears, the unknown no longer feared

From the overflow eye am delivered whole and holy
Cleansed from the persecution of an over imaginative ego
Released from the bondage of my generation's self-hate
Eye smile now because it pleases me to do so

Hope is no longer just a name for pretty little girls
Faith is no longer just the trust and belief in the unseen
Patience is something that eye have learned to treasure
Unconditional love . . . is all . . . that . . . eye have . . . to give . . .

The Heart of a Poet

Sayeed Abubakar, a modern epic-poet of Bengali language, was born on September 21, 1972 in Bangladesh. His first collection of poems, *First Sin of Love*, published in 1996, gave him a considerable popularity in Bangladesh. He continues to write poetry. **His poems have been translated into many languages, such as English, Spanish, Chinese, Russian, Arabic, Persian, Odia, and Malayalam. He was given many literary awards, including the Lalon Award (2009), the DCL Literary Award (2015), the Syed Ali Ahsan Award (2017) and the Indian Rock Pebbles International Literary Award (2017).**

The Last Hope of Earth

From night to day,
Sorrow to peace,
Pride to courtesy,
Hatred to love
Is our journey.

We can't turn back.
We can't stop here.
Man is crying,
Crying children,
Flowers and birds;

Friends, we are the
Last hope of Earth.

Akhmad Cahyo Setio is a literary activist from the Tanah Bumbu Regency of Indonesia. He has participated in various literary activities locally and internationally. His poems appeared in numerous poetry anthologies and presented at festivals nationally and internationally, including *Amaravati Poem Prism* (2018 and 2019, India), *Just Love Me* (2019, Nepal), *International Malays Festival* (2018, Singapore), *International Poems Anthology of Palestine Solidarity* (2018, Malaysia), *World Healing World Peace* (2020, USA), *Azahar Revista Poetica*, Vol. 104 (2020, Spain), *Rendition of International Poetry* (2020, China), and *Poetas Por La Paz Y La Libertad* (2020, Italy).

akhmadcahyosetio@gmail.com
https://akhmadcahyosetio.blogspot.com

The Human Being

If we are not siblings
But remember
We are brothers and sisters
If we are not brothers and sisters
But remember
We are one tribe
If we are not one tribe
But remember
We are countrymen
If we are not countrymen
But remember
We are fellow human beings

So, what is the reason that makes us hate each other,
Divorce to the point of spilling blood between people?

Are I and you different?
I eat you eat too
You drunk, I drunk
I breathe you breathe
You want to live a quiet, happy life
Me too
Then what is different from us?
Until snatch the life of the Almighty

Do you remember, Adam and Eve in heaven?
Shaytan incited envy to them
Then possessed in the form of lust in the chest
Until the punishment applies to them

Do not be deceived, we are wise human beings,
Let's tighten our hands, side by side,
Live happily in the world so that nature is baqa

The Heart of a Poet

Born in a village in South Kashmir, Farooq Ahmad Sheikh has graduated from the University in Srinagar of the Kashmir territory. He earned his Ph.D. from the same university. He was appointed Assistant Professor of English in one of the campuses of the University of Kashmir. Writing and reading have been his fascination since the day he became aware of himself. Life has been a great teacher, but the best books that he aspires to read endlessly are those of the Universe and of his own soul.

Dialogue

There is this unending pain
I craved to ask
But then I saw the deep dazzled eyes
And was lost in them
I gathered some courage and asked
"Where from that light comes?"

"Look for it inside you"
He said as if talking to someone else

"How shall I do that?"
I asked again!

"Seek guidance"
He said

"From who?"
I asked softly

"From the earth
That sustains the life and beauty in life
That does not know what it means to hate
That loves the good and the bad alike
And
From the eagle
To be fearless to fly alone beyond the horizon
To be the determined to conquer the unknown
And
From the bee
That makes honey only to serve its purpose
And remains indifferent to who eats it
And
From the candle
That burns itself to give away light
And

The Heart of a Poet

Finally from the moth
That destroys his being for love
And to be one with love"
He said

"Guide me then"
In seeking guidance"
I asked

"Be a mirror and reflect
Locate yourself in the whole
Discover the whole in you
In the single ray
Search for the whole sun"
He said

"What shall I do with this pain?"
I asked at last

"It is the flame to guide you
To roll your passion into compassion
And to place you on your path"
He said

"Where shall that path lead?"
I asked

"To the door behind which
Same light is waiting to come out"
He said and directed me to leave

The Conscious Poets

Elizabeth Esguerra Castillo is an internationally noted author and poet from the Philippines. She has two books to her credit, *Seasons of Emotions* (UK) and *Inner Reflections of the Muse* (USA), and has contributed to nearly 100 international anthologies with her poems.

Hold on

In an ailing world, hope is still dawning,
With every breath we take
Feel the gratitude
We are all in this together,
Though living apart
We are One.

Hold on to your faith
There's the sun at the horizon,
A new day is about to greet us
After all we've been through,
Love is the only cure.

Hold on, dear One,
The Dove of Peace will fly once more
To bring hope amid the dark clouds,
Hold on to the dream
That one fine day,
We will meet halfway.

The Conscious Poets

An ardent lover of nature, poetry, photography and music, Madhumathi believes that writing is soul's metamorphosis, a kaleidoscopic view of life through words. In her strong belief in the therapeutic power of words, she spreads mental health awareness through writing and takes part in related activities to break the stigma and to reiterate the importance of empathy. Madhumathi's poems have been published in *Poetry Society India*, *Chennai Poetry Circle*, *India Poetry Circle*, and *Poetic Prism*. Muse India (UGC-approved), International Writer's Journal, Science Shore, Our Poetry Archives and Positive Vibes are some of the e-zines in which her poems have appeared.

Handheld by Hope

Upon the garden of our heart, when hope gently rains
Quenching the parched roots
Dressing our desolate wounds
Pulling our soul
To dance in the rain
Life blooms in vibrant hues
Zest for life, perfuming our dreams and tomorrows
It is never too late
To learn to love life
With bouquets of hope . . .
If a handful of smiles
We could gift a few aching souls
A portion of their heart, we could heal
Pages from the past, one fears to revisit
If we could go with them, holding hands
Meet and remove the weeds of nightmares
Clean the cobwebs of guilt and shame
Hear them pour out their unheard stories, and
Come back with replenished hearts
With more sun, and space for happier tomorrows
If we could be a tiny reason
For hope sprouting in hearts
Smiles blooming in souls
We have not lived in vain
If words could plant hope, and heal
If poems could sprout as elixir
Let our heart, and soul
Melt as ink and flow as words
To heal the broken, to shoulder the lonely
Wipe the tears, of torn survivors . . .
Every word each syllable
May it blossom announcing the arrival of spring
For all the lives, trapped in autumn
It is never how big
But, with how much love we do

The Conscious Poets

Our little acts of kindness . . .
To a heart brimming with hope
Let 'Giving' add shine and sparkle
Giving, is joy, a humbling Metamorphosis
A handful of smiles, are all that is needed
To make the world a paradise . . .
A handful of poems, is all we need
To paint the world with love
In a myriad of hues of hope
Leaving heart prints, and stencils of gratitude behind . . .

The Heart of a Poet

From Kerala, India, Seena Sreevalson is a bilingual poet, translator, an editor and a classical dancer who experiments with the visual aspects of poetry. She writes in English and Malayalam. She has presented her poems in several national and international poetry festivals, and some have been published in international poetry anthologies. She has compiled and edited two international anthologies of English poems, *The Current and Global poetry* (from 40 nations across the globe) and two editions of *Prime Poetry Festival* (Kerala, 2019 and 2020). She was awarded the Poonthanam Yuva Sahithya Puraskaram prize for her anthology in Malayalam.

Eternal

Start a new dawn of life
To place our being in nature.
Let love spread its wings
Far away in the cosmic world
To light up wonders.
Merge with the colours of trees
Rhythm of rivers.
Swim with fish
Dive into the blue sea.
Fly with a bird
Know the heights of mountain peaks,
Be silent.
Sharp your ears.
Listen . . .
Fluttering of butterflies,
Music of the bamboo forest,
Inhale . . .
Smell of wild flowers.
The nature you seek is within.
Green is not a simple word.
Know the ways of nature
Feel the Green.

The Heart of a Poet

Dr. Nirmal Jaswal is a bilingual poet, short story writer, translator and critic. She has received several awards, notably the Best Book of the Year prize from Chandigarh Sahit Academy, REIT ka Rishta (2013), Angaar (2014), and NAZAAKTAN (2017). She also is a recipient of the 2001 Best Woman award from Barnala and a 2006 fellowship from the Punjabi Academy in Leicester, UK. Her poetry collection was launched in 2019 and another is in progress. She has 14 books to her credit and has travelled widely in connection with her literary pursuits.

Imprisoned Life

Life never stops
Hope is never lost
When there's passion
life grows
even in a glass jar
Life never stops

For how long
the lockdown would last
For how long
the doors would be kept closed
For how long
there would be hurdles in our paths
My ancestral Banyan tree
is just a stump
But it's not alone
It's swaying in the breeze
Oh! Now it's breathing afresh

You may imprison us
But one day
with open arms
We will awaken
The greenery
would sprout
even in a glass jar
It would spread
would teach humans
a good lesson
How to live a good life
How to live on this earth

The Heart of a Poet

Noreen Ann Snyder is a poet who has four collections of poems to her credit. Three of them have been co-authored with her loving husband, Garry A. Snyder. She will always do what she can to honor him, and keep his spirit alive. In his honor, she created The Poetry Club and Facebook Live that is active every Saturday evening.

Be a Thorn

Be different
Don't be a follower
be a leader
that everyone will
respect, honor, and love.
Be you
Stand up and be counted.
Be a thorn
in someone's side.
Let that person know
it isn't right.
Don't be afraid . . .
Don't be afraid of the bully.
Be a thorn in the bully's side.
Speak up and be heard!
Speak up . . .
Be a thorn
without violence and abuse.

Zia Marshall is a Learning Designer and Communication Specialist with an M.A. and Ph.D. in English Literature. She is skilled in performance and competency development for personal and professional growth and has designed a course on Time Management for Productivity and Work-Life Balance at Udemy. A member of the India Poetry Circle, she is passionate about writing. Her work has been featured in the e-zine, Adelaide Literary Magazine, the *Quarterly Literary Review of Singapore*, *Contemporary Literary Journal of India* and the *Scarlet Leaf Review*. She was a finalist in the Adelaide Literary Awards in 2018 and 2019.

http://www.selfgrowth.com/
https://elearningindustry.com/

The Pink-rimmed Dawn of Hope

The flaming torch of the setting sky
The Blue Hour betwixt day and night
Twilight heralds cosmic dichotomy
Your Animagus spews poison or honey

The Mystic Hour chants sacred rites
Whispered promises of a new light
Rousing souls from the nocturnal sea
Towards the sparkling light of eternity

As dawn breaks in the pink-rimmed sky
Hope eternal spirals high
Buds blossom from blackened plague
A new life, we celebrate!

Earth, it's now your turn to breathe
Flowers blossom under verdant leaves
Birds soar free in cerulean skies
And people remember how to smile

Dolphins frolic in the aqua seas
Nature dances in cosmic symphony
People shed old ways for new
Love and kindness are given their due

The charred soil blooms anew
Gratitude blossoms, relationships renew
Healing light spills like mellifluous rain
Dawn sky heralds let's begin again!

The Heart of a Poet

Born in South Kalimantan, Indonesia, Hatmiati Masy'ud is active in scientific writings. Her short stories and poems have appeared in numerous publications, including *Downtime Catching Wind* (2013), *When Back in Love* (a joint anthology, 2014), *Galuh Floating Market* (with Aliansyah Jumbawuya, 2016), *Sun Picking Women* (joint anthology, 2016), *Mandi Bungas* (joint anthology, 2017), *Pilanggur* (a Banjar anthology, 2017) – which received the 2018 Literature Rancage award, *Selendang Mayang* (joint anthology, 2017), and *Bacina Buta* (a Banjar anthology, 2020). She is often asked to give a speech at various gatherings related to culture, literature, and language.

hatmiati.masyud@gmail.com

Peace

The time runs following season
The sun rises and sets every time
The one behavior is very verse
Leaved a trail of steps

The universe is like rug
Make a peace and creates of tenderness
Then the beauty of soul eternity
And we had a lot of fun

The spirit feels wholeheartedly
Open the hope and going success
In the line release a charm
Reached happy with love

Mallika Chari, a poet and an artist, loves to give colours and shape to her poetry. Her poetry collection, *Lively Words* bears testimony to this where each of her poem is represented by her paintings. Her poems have found places in online journals and print poetry anthologies. Her haiga and haiku have been published in edited e-zines.

The Spirit-Secret of Survival

Sand castles are built to pass time,
Castles in mind are built on
Possessed resolutions.

A slide is charming,
A fall is cherished further,
Time passes playfully.

When a small slide itself is paralyzing,
Can a collapse be survived!
Time stacks up severely.

Still,
Summoned to subdue the shortfalls,
Stabilized soul surrenders not;
Spirit of making sand castles
Shoots up further;
Surpassed success survives again!
And
The strengthened soul salutes "Thee" for
Solemnly sowing a strong mind!

Originally from Kolkata, Shamayita Sen is currently based in Delhi, India. She has a Ph.D. in English and is a research scholar in the Department of English at the University of Delhi. Her interest in teaching and academic research centers around British modernism, contemporary Anglophone literature, Indian political literature and the theories on body, violence, trauma and gender. She has been writing poetry since her college days in Kolkata. Her poems have been published in *Muse India*, *WE View* and in other international poetry anthologies.

Afternoons

With an afternoon of dull pain all to myself
I ran across the coastline in search of shells
that tell stories of a past I revisit
most nights as soon as the Wi-Fi goes numb
post news of bombings in Gaza or Kashmir,
that is, if laying upon my lazy back I can
scoop up news amidst this censorship.
On other afternoons or moonless evenings
we flock into the dinning room awaiting fish curry
surfing through dance videos, reality TV or Bollywood
skirting well past international news that might
curse children with sleeplessness or anxiety attacks.

Yesterday I overheard stories of a mango tree
I used to stare at on vacation afternoons.
Now we have neither the courtyard nor the tree.
I wonder if I was ever allowed to build a swing of
ropes that lay waste of the monthly deliveries
from our factory. I remember blind negotiations
among uncles who laid bare neither their soul
nor their past while auctioning our childhood memories
to strangers who never visited the courtyard later.

Sometimes I wonder how international news
sediments beneath clutter of family life:
a storehouse of never to be used things,
utensils clanging not as a sign of protest and hunger,
but as sounds of festivity in a country
where only 9% of the population
skim their morning milk as preparation
to sieve daily life through work-days.

These lonely afternoons are special.
One can revisit ghosts of a world less traveled or be
transported to another through images and sketches or
flip a coin to know one's sole desire through
moments of utter dilemma – all in the hope
of a hunger-free world saved of its intermittent bombings.

The Heart of a Poet

Born in 1977, Tara Noesantara (Andaru Ratnasari) lives in Surabaya (East Java) and Yogyakarta (Central Java), Indonesia. She claims to have just wrestled with poetry, but her literary culture-specific essays can be seen in *Jawa Post*, *Surabaya Post*, and *Kedaulatan Rakyat*. She has provided poetry anthologies for young adults with a foreword several times. She frequently works on short stories and novels which have been transformed into mini theater plays. She loves the world of dance and acting, both of which started at the Zero Theater (Teater Nol) and the Theater Institute Surabaya (Teater Institut Surabaya).

Don't Break It . . .

Don't mourn my woman.
because that disaster will subside your heart.
Wear your masks because you still have a million colors.
Hi, don't cry my woman because the tempest will disappear, straighten up your steps
because you still have a charm.
Smile, my woman.
because your lanterns will light the world.
Sing my woman.
song dawn is cheerful with the birds singing,
recede the true nature of who you are . . .

The Heart of a Poet

Dr. Queen Sarkar is a multilingual poet, translator and an academic in Ranchi, India. She has earned her Ph.D. from IIT in Kharagpur. Her review articles, research papers and poetry have been published in reputed international journals and anthologies. Her poems have been translated into Spanish, Arabic and Gujarati. Sarkar has been appointed as the "Ambassador of Good Will Seeds of Youth XXI Century" and the "United Nations of Letters – Uniletras" in India and is the Ambassador of Peace for Switzerland / France. Sarkar is also a member of the World Nations Writer's Union of Kazakhstan.

Petals of Hope

Petals of hope,
Growing through dirt,
Each bearing the pigments of the past.

Colors?

Choleric, melancholic, phlegmatic, sanguine,
carrying the weight of hunger, anger, yearning and fatigue.

Scudded across the iridescent clouds,
my heart beats like thunder with lilac lightning.

Flag for some, fabric with ink for others,
Marching with pride, creating history of honour.

Petals of hope,
Facing adversity;
Each ribbon tangled with awareness.

Ribbons?

Pink, black, green, purple and red.
Bright spots of hope, in dark situations,
Cancer, AIDS, Apraxia, Child Abuse, Sex Trafficking and fight against autism.

Stemming from the wedding roots, unwrapping birth,
cutting the ceremonial ribbon, enjoying the gardens of earthy mirth.

Restrictions for some, opportunities for others.
United in solidarity, together in distance, let's celebrate the power of non-violence.

Writing is a spiritual journey for Teresa E. Gallion. Her passions are traveling and hiking on the mountains and in the desert landscapes of New Mexico's sacred grounds. Her journeys into nature are nurtured by the Sufi poets Rumi and Hafiz. She has three books to her credit, *Walking Sacred Ground, Contemplation in the High Desert*, and *Chasing Light*. The latter was a finalist in the 2013 New Mexico / Arizona Book Awards. Her poems have appeared in numerous journals and anthologies.

http://teresagallion.yolasite.com/

The Hope Pony

The Hope Pony runs in the wilderness
wild and free and your last chance
to hitch a ride is still possible.

Ground rules do apply.
Faith is required to enter the woods.
Love must create a flame around you.

If the rules are observed,
Hope runs right into the flame
lighting the road to salvation.

The next phase of your life begins.
Resistance cannot stop hope
when the flame of love burns.

The Heart of a Poet

The poet and author Muhammad Azram hails from Pakistan. He has emerged in the literary world with no formal institutional background, yet he stands firm on the grounds of art and literature. He cultivates his zest through his flowing ideas into the fertile soils of poetry, seeking to connect with life's inner dialogues and monologues. His writings continue to be published widely, and his poems reside in various international anthologies and magazines. His work has been translated into Spanish, French, Serbian and other languages. He is a member of a number of literary organizations and the recipient of many international awards and honors.

Hope Rules Life

I am surrounded
by pains, hopelessness,
disappointments
And darkness
Yet, whenever
I sit to write about life
With my pen
Words, phrases and lines
Start flying like birds
of hope, light, and life
Two show me diverse
Colors of life
Which makes me believe
Hope rules on hopelessness
Light rules on darkness
And life rules everything
that is related to life
And
Life is greater
than anything else
Even though
it is surrounded by
distraction and disorientation
Yet
Hope is ruling life
Life is ruling everything else

The Heart of a Poet

Born in Leon Guanajuato, Mexico in 1977, Fernando Martinez Alderete is a writer, poet, theater actor, and radio producer. He has one poetry book, *El despertar de las hadas* and one collection of short stories, *DOCEHORAS DE UN POETA EN EL MAR* to his credit. His poems have been published in 63 anthologies in thirteen countries around the world.

For a Future

What will come with the future?
New ways to love us?
No apathy for giving us
hand without a rush.
Destroying selfishness,
not coveting riches,
enjoying the simplicities
of flowers and realism.
Enjoy the fresh air,
touching people with longing,
of a kiss without suspicion
with a safe hug.
They will vaccinate against anger,
against power struggles,
great pleasures will return
to help the one who looks at us.
We will enjoy friends,
we will conquer viruses
praying we will fight
forgiving enemies.

The Heart of a Poet

Born in 1961 to a Catholic family, Yanz Haryo Darmista lives in the Yogyakarta region of Central Java, Indonesia. Theater, poetry and painting have been his passion from junior high school on. He has worked as a journalist, managing short stories, poetry, art, culture and tourism in the *Gapura Yogyakarta* tabloid. After joining the Yogyakarta Alam Theater with performances in Sophocles' *Oedipus Trilogy*, *Oedipus Rex*, *Colonus* and *Antigone*, Albert Camus' *Caligula*, and Samuel Beckett's *Waiting for Godot*, Yanz performed in Malaysia, Singapore, the Philippines and Bangkok. He trains college students in theater at the Sanata Darma University in Yogyakarta.

My Step-Contained Past

Evening with star jewels
I sing the song of hope
When my soul drifts in the remnants of the remnants of the past
The sound is soft and lips are trembling in a fragile body
My step came to the debris of the sun's monument
A long and tiring journey
I fell on a barren grass
I cry because of my weakness . . .
I screamed and my heart ached
to tell my dreams of the past
In a step of beauty
who had left my footing . . .
My tears dripped like blood oozing from wounds
I complained and sobbed painfully
Because of the loneliness that is isolated from my tribe
Should I hold a grudge
Who walks between the walls of hatred . . .
I love my heart even though the judge is weak
But weakness sustains my hope
In search of light for darkness
I don't know when and where that light won over me . . .

The Heart of a Poet

Born in 1950, Asoke Kumar Mitra is from Kolkata, India. He has two poetry books to his credit, *Savage Wind* and *Song of Pebbles*.

Let Us . . .

Let us close our eyes
Before this loneliness
Shadows running into the summer wind

Language of hope
A magic voyage
Dragonfly goes wild

Fugitive wind
And the sunflower in our closed eyes
Broken memories of years gone by

Escaping nameless darkness
Fireflies dancing
Moving Silently towards morning sun

Only a poet knows
The heart of a poet
Whispers of a crazy sea wind . . .

The Heart of a Poet

Kay Salady is an author who is based in Washington. She is an activist for peace, and has participated in anthologies and online magazines to this end.

A Poet's Heart

A poet's heart is empathetic
For he walks a path of peace
His mind is contemplative
He sees what lies beneath
The hardened outer clay
To the very soul of man
He cries out for the world
Trying so to understand
In the silence of the night
He searches for the words
His attempt to make things right
So that others might be heard
But are mere words enough
This blood poured on the page
To make you understand
That hope lies in the sage

The Heart of a Poet

Ameedah Mawalin is originally from Chicago. Her mission is healing the world and her community through creativity for stress management. She began her spoken word journey in 1993 with performances from 1996 on. To date, she dishes out her signature piece, "Midnight Brew" from her book, *Ebony Sonnets* upon popular request. The piece was inspired by her mentor, Regie Gibson of the film *Love Jones* upon attending his poetry workshop. Ameedah was awarded the Firekeeper Award in 2019 by P.O.E.T (People of Extraordinary Talent) and the Midwest Professional Empire, LLC.

www.sapphirewithpassion.com

Cast a Spell

Cast a spell of charm and grace, and grant some patience too.
Cast a spell of time and space, to learn and grow anew.

Cast a spell of noble chance, to inspire, teach, and train.
Cast a spell of rhythm and dance
to calm and soothe your pain.

Cast a spell of charm and wit, to tantalize and perceive.
Cast a spell of hard work and grit, to persist and achieve.

Cast a spell of honor and respect, of others near and far.
Cast a spell to consider and reflect
on what you'll become or are.

Cast a spell of vision and sight, to realize all your dreams.
Cast a spell of strength, hope, and might,
for the Lord (MIND) hath power over all things!

The Heart of a Poet

Writer, freelance journalist and housewife, Nandita De nee Chatterjee is the Consulting Editor of *Environ*; worked at *Economic Times*; wrote the cover stories and features for *Statesman, Illustrated Weekly, Economic Times, Telegraph, Times of India, Femina, Filmfare, Germany Today, Voix Meets Mode UK, Frontier Weekly* and *Namaste Ink*, and has launched *Economic Times Marketplace*. She has been working as a part-time lecturer in the Journalism Department of Calcutta University for the last 7 months. Nandita is the co-author of numerous books, including *Big Bang of Non-Fiction, Life in Reverse, 30 Best Poets, Sea, Coffee & Echos,* and *Wrapped Up Feelings*.

The Year of Conviction

2080.
A serene summer afternoon.
The bright teenager pulls up his chair.
Grandpa, you lived through the worst pandemic of the world.
How did humanity survive?

Looking out into the glorious sunlight,
watching shadows of dancing blades of cycad,
lines in his temple standing out,
a gentle voice replies,
'On hope, my child.'

2020.
A summer such as none.
A winter which brought calamity without a warning.
Overnight a contagion swept through nations.
Wiping out the seemingly healthy.
A dystopian tale suddenly taking shape,
a real world, unreal fate.
Unknown enemy, killer virus.
Felling weak and strong.
Unknown remedies.

'The wisest went to work.
Scientists, doctors,
governments, institutions,
man to man they held hands.
Implicit faith, inbuilt belief in themselves.
Health workers across the world
working overtime on the ground.
Best brains cooped up behind walls
labouring incessantly.
One objective, one combined effort.
Beyond borders, beyond differences.
Sharing every resource existing.
It was a world where the cerebral took charge.
Divisions and divisive forces were forgotten.
A new future for humanity envisioned.
A planet for the children

The Heart of a Poet

sustainable, salubrious,
human, social, economic, environmental sustenance,
foundations laid to revert damages.
Lessons from scourges of the past relearned.
Respect to the elements
gratitude to the universe.
Reaffirmation of reverence to life.

'Introspection, application,
resources unearthed.
Valiant efforts at every individual level.
Man learned to be responsible.
Caring, sharing, protecting,
praying for a better day.
At every platform human goodness unfolded.
Futility of apathy, hatred, bias
reinforced in one severe lesson.

'It was a summer of unprecedented challenges.
It was the time when strength of mind
battled the invisible.
Unforeseen circumstances,
formidable efforts.
Humanity raised its bars
will to survive
new frontiers in medicine
new ethics,
a new ethos for life.
On the pillars of hope
humanity came together
to build a new world,
bulwarked against mistakes old.'

The shadows lengthened.
The elderly gentleman became silent.
The planet had revived.
Man had learned the hard way.
Natural and manmade disasters plenty.
But united humanity had learned to survive.

The Conscious Poets

The CEO and founder of Queendom Network, Sylvia L. Blalock, aka DarkJoyChyld, was born in San Francisco, California. She hates writing bios, though she loves writing. She has authored and published *Uprising: a Book of Poetry*, and has an upcoming fantasy novel, *Sista: How Skynet Sparked The Revolution*. A book of life lessons, tentatively titled *This Is Why We Don't Get Invited To The Cookout* as well as a number of video, graphic design and poetry projects are on her radar.

www.sblalock.com
www.uprising-radio.com
www.queendom.network

Dear Life

My alarm went off, as usual at 4:45 AM . . .
I have a job that I don't have to log into, today.
I have a morning to wake up early to.
There is a sunrise happening with violet streaks of personal promise
In my mind's heart's eyes
I see you out there, world.
When I can return to you
CORONA CLEARED
AND YOU TO ME THE SAME
I would pull you into a
Far too long overdue
Deep embrace
That we should hold onto each other for dear life
Having now learned just how truly dear we each are to life
Oh, dear life
If you would still have me,
I will cherish each and every
Remaining moment of it
In honor of those who breathed
Their last taste of it
Alone, yet dearly loved
In a war
Still waging itself around them.
. . . BREATHING LOVE, LIFE AND LIGHT
To those who volunteered to fight
A seen enemy
And today's armies fighting for us all
Right now.
Those enemies
Seen and unseen

A native of Turkey, hülya n. yılmaz [sic] is Liberal Arts Emerita (The Pennsylvania State University, USA), Co-Chair and Director of Editing Services at Inner Child Press International, tri-lingual writer, literary translator, professional book evaluator and reviewer, and ghost writer. She has six poetry books to her credit, one of which has been co-authored. Her poetry has appeared in various anthologies of global endeavors. hülya [sic] finds it vital for everyone to understand a deeper sense of self, and writes creatively to attain a comprehensive awareness for our humanity.

https://hulyanyilmaz.com/

problem-free

a new day is dawning tenderly
on rainbow-hued and ocean-scented sheets

the laughter of countless infants
appears on mouthwatering breakfast trays

our screen-free window is always wide open
it invites in the freshly-breeding families of house wrens
their united eyes watch their yet-to-be-hatched eggs
tap dance on cue – uninhibited and carefree
the matured ones chant the elating news the wind brings
amid a gentlest breeze – putting all worries at ease
the resulting love-songs taste like chilled lemonade
on a day of a hottest summer's blaze

the world has just been declared a problem-free zone

The Conscious Poets

William S. Peters, Sr., aka 'Just Bill', is an award-winning global activist for humanity. His poetry and prowess have been acknowledged and translated across the world. He is the founder and chair of Inner Child Enterprises, Inner Child Press International and the World Healing, World Peace Foundation. He utilizes these vehicles along with his poetry and other writings to champion the cause of consciousness, peace, love, acceptance and compassion. His personal perspective is that 'life is a garden', and we must plant seeds of good intent, light and love that we all may harvest a sweet bountiful fruit. The 'by-line' Mr. Peters has coined for Inner Child Press International is 'building bridges of cultural understanding'. Achieving this vital connection is his inspiration.

For the Day to Come

In the playgrounds
And fields of play,
Where the children play
Without any cares
Of the morrow,
We, the guardians
Of the time to come
Must work diligently
Maintain the vigil
To give them the world
They deserve

The children of today
Shall someday inherit
That which we leave
Behind . . .
And we must expect more
Of ourselves,
For there is more
Within us
Than we have demonstrated
Thus far

We must let go
Of our trust
In the wrong things,
And focus
On our hearts,
And live from
Our Holy center,
And allow the light of love
To enter

We must laugh more,
Sing more,

The Conscious Poets

Dance more,
Listen more,
Share more,
Be more,
That we may even
The 'Karmic' score
Of our existence . . .
And we will,
For the day to come
Is nearly upon us,
And cannot be avoided

Inner Child Press International

Inner Child Press International is a publishing company founded and operated by writers. Our personal publishing experiences provide us an intimate understanding of the sometimes-daunting challenges writers, new and seasoned, may face in the business of publishing and marketing their creative "Written Work".

For more Information:

Inner Child Press International

www.innerchildpress.com
intouch@innerchildpress.com

'building bridges of cultural understanding'
www.innerchildpress.com